Meow!

My Groovy Life with *Tiger Beat*'s Teen Idols

Ann Moses

with Ann Wicker

MEOW! MY GROOVY LIFE WITH TIGER BEAT'S TEEN IDOLS

Formatted by: Carol Davis

Cover designer: Steven Novak

Dedication

To the superstars in my best life –
my husband Tony, and my sons, Matt and Mike.
You have made my life better than any Disney fantasy.

TABLE OF CONTENTS

Introduction

By Bobby Sherman

It was, after all, 1970. No Twitter, no websites, no email. Bags of fan mail five feet high arriving at the studio every day—no possible way to read or answer them. How to respond to tens of thousands of fans, mostly girls in their early teens, some who wrote every day? They really needed to hear back from me.

There were two monthly fan magazines. *16* was in New York. But *Tiger Beat* was here in Hollywood. More accurately, *Tiger Beat*, in the person of Ann Moses, was on the set, in the studio, and part of my life.

I didn't realize how young Ann was, but it didn't take long to recognize that her instincts for what the fans wanted, and what I wanted for them, were perfect.

Looking back, maybe "Peace, Love and Bobby Sherman," "Win Bobby's Choker Neck Band," "Have Lunch with Bobby" or

"Bobby Sherman: I'll Never Lie to You!" were a little breathless. But the fundamental message in every issue was that I loved, cared for, and respected my fans, and that they should feel the same way about themselves at a crucial time in their lives.

And now I finally get to read Ann writing about Ann, not about me. It's about time.

Peace and Love,

SO GOOD TO HEAR from you, ANN!
BE WELL & SAFE!

Bobby

February 3, 1968

It's my twenty-first birthday. I'm standing at the front window of my house a block below the Hollywood sign, wearing a dress made especially for me by a woman who designs clothes for famous people. I'm staring out the window, biting my nails, and I'm trying not to cry.

In the kitchen, the phone is ringing. It's been ringing all day long, with calls from movie stars, TV actors, and pop singers who want me to know they're thinking of me today. A few minutes ago, a gal whose new song was climbing the pop charts last week phoned from New York to sing me "Happy Birthday." The prettiest man on television sent two dozen roses. My mailbox at my *Tiger Beat* office was stuffed with greetings from a galaxy of pop stars. Most of these cards, I knew, had been signed by secretaries.

Any other girl in the world would be thrilled with this kind of attention. Any other girl would be thrilled to be me—I know, because every day I get letters from girls all over the country, writing to tell me how much they want to be me. My life is so glamorous, they tell me, because I get to do what they only dream of: hanging out all day with Davy-Bobby-Peter-Dino-Mark-Micky. I'm so lucky, they need me to know, so pretty, so everything-I-want-to-be. I have it all, according to my friends, because all those yummy, smooth-faced young men every girl in America is lusting after are my friends, at least according to the two million readers of *Tiger Beat*, where I've worked since I was barely out of high school.

Oh, yeah? Today, minutes before the big birthday bash my parents are throwing so my friends can meet my rock-star boyfriend, I've never been more unhappy in my life. My heart is broken, thanks to this man who will eventually sell more than 200 million records and be lauded for changing the face of popular music. For now, he's just a handsome singer in a popular rock band, admired by his peers and filling the daydreams of a million other girls—thanks in part to the stories I've written and published about him and his equally pretty brothers. Stories all about how gorgeous his eyes are, how much he adores cuddly kittens and perfect sunny days, and how deeply he loves all his fans—especially *you*!

Especially me! Or so I thought. He swore he loved me, even after he told me—on the night before my birthday!—that he's married and can't see me again.

So much for sunshine and kittens.

I feel the tears coming on again, just as his limousine pulls up. And then I can't help myself: Instead of crying, I laugh. The image of a block-long black Cadillac stopping in front of my humble little house in the Hollywood hills suddenly strikes me as hilarious. And while I watch my rock star ex-boyfriend—just last night, the love of my life!—trudge up my front walkway, I'm thinking to myself, "Good lord, Annie. How in the world did you ever wind up here?"

Chapter 1

Uncle Walt, I Want to Be a Writer

I blame Walt Disney.

Not long after I met the man who "made dreams come true," the stars began to align in my brand-new writing career.

In 1965, I was working as head counter girl at the Sunkist orange juice booth in Adventureland at Disneyland. I was usually the first counter girl on duty and, one June morning at around 7 a.m., I looked up from wiping a counter to find Walt Disney standing in front of me.

"Good morning, Uncle Walt," I said, remembering the Disney University orientation rule to call Mr. Disney either Walt or Uncle Walt.

"You must be Ann," he smiled after glancing at my nametag.

I nodded, speechless. He gave me a great big grin and asked, "May I have an orange juice, please?"

"Large or small?" I squeaked out before shakily turning the spigot and filling a cup. Normally an outgoing, talkative girl, I had a total brain-freeze at the sight of this famous man. As I handed him his cup of juice, I blurted out, "I've written two articles for the Disneyland Employee Newsletter!"

I can't imagine how I expected him to respond to my declaration, but he kindly asked me, "You're a writer?"

Again, I nodded.

"Well, keep it up, Ann," he said. "You never know where it's going to take you."

Then, as casually as he'd appeared, he walked away.

I stood there, motionless, still stunned by what had just happened. There was such energy around Walt Disney, both intimidating and inspiring.

"Well, keep it up, Ann," I whispered to myself. It sounded like fairy dust and magic.

Sure enough, things started happening for me not long after my visit from Uncle Walt.

* * *

In 1965, I was like most every other teenaged girl of the time: virginal, wholesome, absolutely innocent. The only difference between me and every other eighteen-year-old in the United States was my job at *Tiger Beat* magazine, one of the largest teen fan magazines in the country. But before I began hobnobbing with pop stars and actors, I was just an average kid, born in Long Beach, California to Rosemary and Jackson Moses in 1947. We lived in nearby Compton until I was seven, when my father decided he wanted to move his family to the "country" and bought a house in Anaheim.

Our new house was the typical post-war tract home, built in a former orange grove and surrounded on three sides by citrus trees, a single orange tree left in the front yard of each home. The house was a single level ranch with three bedrooms, one-and-a-half baths, and a detached garage covered in Bougainvillea vine.

A lot has been said about this, but it's just the simple truth: Post-war America was a more innocent place and time. No one locked their front doors at night. All the kids on my street played together, rode bikes, roller skated in the driveways, and sometimes snuck two blocks over to the railroad tracks, where we'd lay pennies to be flattened when a freight train roared past. It was safe to spend the entire day playing in the orange groves or walking a half-mile to the elementary school to swing on the monkey bars. In junior high, we built our own skateboards from bits of two-by-fours and the wheels from old roller skates.

I was a good student, but I struggled with writing. I could never get that first sentence down on paper. I had a history report due on Theodore Roosevelt, and although I had made an outline and written research notes, I just could not get started. This was the one time my mom, who was always available to answer a question or help me with homework, sat down and wrote that first sentence for me. I got an "A" on the report and after that gained the courage to never be "stuck" by words or storytelling ever again.

In eighth grade, I applied to be the school reporter for our local daily newspaper, the *Anaheim Bulletin.* The back page of the features section in each Friday edition printed reports from the junior and senior high schools by a reporter from each school. We wrote stories about students who'd excelled in something, or covered a student dance. I was paid fifteen cents a column inch, so I wrote lots of stories.

In high school, I was sports editor of the yearbook in my junior year and promoted to editor my senior year. I was also on the Songleading squad that year. Unlike the cheerleaders, who wore knee-length pleated skirts and long-sleeved wool sweaters, we followed the marching band out onto the field at the beginning of each football game in thigh-high dresses with flared skirts and majorette boots. We performed dance routines with pom-poms each time the band played a fight song. I was also active in the school's Tri-Hi-Y group, a YMCA affiliate that did fundraisers. I was a member of the Girls Athletic Association.

In my pre-teen years, summers were boring. We played "school" a lot in the garage. At my friend Kerry's house, we dug "the Mississippi River," a mud hole about two feet deep and fifteen yards long which we filled with "river" water, and proceeded to get muddy from head to toe. I didn't receive an allowance back then, and neither did my brother, Jack, eighteen months older than I and a year ahead in school. I'd volunteer to clean my parents' garage in exchange for twenty-five cents. Or, even though I hated it, I'd wash all the outside windows of the house for fifty cents. When they tore down the orange grove south of our tract to build more homes, Jack and I sold iced tea to the carpenters working there. One summer, I worked as a camp counselor at a day camp. It beat cleaning the garage.

Shortly after we moved to Anaheim, the *Bulletin* announced that Walt Disney had purchased 160 acres and was breaking ground on an amusement park there. Disneyland would be located exactly two miles from our house, and we often made the short drive down to the construction site to watch it going up from a distance. At first, all we could see were tall wooden fences as the underground portion was constructed, but as time went on, we saw the turrets of Sleeping Beauty's Castle and enormous trees and palms that would become part of Adventureland. Disneyland opened on July 17, 1955.

My brother Jack was only ten, but he got a job at Disneyland that first summer, selling a daily newspaper called *Disneyland News* alongside his friend Steve. The paper listed what time the band would march down Main Street and any other special attractions happening that day, and included a map of the park. Later, Jack and Steve sold guidebooks for the park. Because the entrance was just outside of Main Street USA, my mom sewed turn-of-the-century striped jackets for the boys to wear. Jack got to keep ten cents from each guidebook sold. My brother saved all his money because he wanted to buy his first car when he turned sixteen, but Steve spent every penny of his earnings at the Magic Shop on Main Street. Steve had other plans: He wanted to be in show business. His last name was Martin, and he launched his legendary stand-up career wearing a hat with an arrow through it that he probably bought at the Magic Shop at Disneyland.

I joined the guys at Disneyland in June of 1962 as a Sunkist counter girl, and I loved every minute of working there. My employee pass allowed me to hang out at Disneyland whenever I wanted, and I could usually ride one of the rides without a ticket if I wore my employee badge. Back then, you could get on a pack mule in Frontierland and travel through the "Painted Desert" full of real cacti. That area was later transformed into Big Thunder Mountain Railroad.

In later years, I often used my employee pass to go into the park on Saturday nights because Kay Bell and the Spacemen, a rock band, were playing in Tomorrowland. All the local high school kids met there on Saturday nights and danced the Watusi and the Pony. Out of town guests to Disneyland were often shocked at our gyrations, but we had a complete blast.

I was also moonlighting on summer weeknights at Melodyland Theatre, located across the street from Disneyland, as a volunteer usher. Melodyland was a popular tourist attraction and a staple for the locals to see the road shows of Broadway musicals like *Annie Get Your Gun* and *Oklahoma!* The stage was circular, and the seats surrounded the stage—there were no bad seats in the house. If you'd seen the show and wanted to go home after everyone was seated, that was okay, too. I saw a lot of musicals for free.

One July night in 1965, I showed up for work at Melodyland to discover that a rock 'n' roll concert was scheduled. The headliners were the Dave Clark Five, and the opening acts were the Astronauts, the Premiers, and a new duo I hadn't heard of named Sonny and Cher. There were two shows, one at 5 p.m. and one at 9 p.m.

I knew the DC5's big hits "Glad All Over" and "Bits and Pieces." The British Invasion was in full swing, and all my friends were crazy about the Beatles. Anything with long hair and a British accent was hot, and the DC5, with their sharply tailored suits, were the first of the big UK bands to play here. As I watched them perform, all I could think was, "Wow! I've *got* to meet these guys."

While they were still on stage, I noticed a man standing near the stage door. He looked official and was closely watching the guys perform. I knew he was the guy I needed to speak to.

"Hello, I'm Ann Moses."

He seemed annoyed by my interruption, but he gave me a small smile. "Hello, Ann, I'm Rick Picone, the DC5's tour manager." His focus returned to the band.

I forged ahead. “I’m the editor of the Fullerton Junior College newspaper, and I’ve been assigned to write an article on the Dave Clark Five. When will be a good time to interview them?”

While I really was the co-editor of the newspaper, I had made up the “assignment” bit on the spot.

He looked at me, quite amused, and said, “Ann, the boys are busy doing two shows tonight. That just won’t be possible.”

I could tell he felt bad about turning me away. I decided to give it one more try. “Rick, I only need five minutes with the band. Can you make it happen for me?”

Rick stared at me and smiled—this time a big grin. I know he was tickled by my nerve.

“Okay, Ann. Tell you what,” he said, grabbing a piece of paper and scribbling on it. He handed it to me. “Come back at 7 p.m., and I’ll give you five minutes for a quick interview with the band. They’re going to be tired and eating dinner, so you won’t have much time. Give backstage security this note.”

I looked down at the note in my hand, which read: *To whom it may concern: Please admit this young lady. Rick Picone, Manager, Dave Clark Five.*

I was ecstatic. I wanted to scream and tell the entire audience that in a couple of hours I was going to be sitting only an arm’s length away from these darling boys.

I tried not to behave like a teenybopper fan, but my excitement was so overwhelming that I threw my arms around

Rick and gave him a huge hug. I ran to the parking lot, jumped into my parents' 1955 Ford sedan, and drove the two miles home as fast as I could. I screamed as I opened the front door, "I've got to change! I'm interviewing the Dave Clark Five in an hour!"

I got cleaned up, put on my best dress, fixed my hair, and grabbed my notepad, pen, my tape recorder, and my camera.

Right up until then, watching the DC5 in action, I had never had a desire to meet any "stars." Oh, I had dreamt of meeting James Darren after seeing the first *Gidget* movie, but that was fan worship from afar. I wanted to be a *real* journalist; it was, after all, my major in college. Never in my wildest dreams did I imagine I'd wind up with a writing career interviewing celebrities. That night, my path took a wild turn in an unexpected direction. Once I got back to the theater, I was apprehensive as I approached the backstage door. This was my first time backstage at a rock concert. I was worried I'd get tongue-tied once I was close to these oh-so-cute guys. Once I was inside, Rick gave me a comforting smile and put me at ease as best he could, then led me to the band's dressing room door.

"All right, boys, let's give Miss Ann a few minutes for an interview."

Five very handsome young men stared at me: Dave Clark, Michael Smith, Lenny Davidson, Rick Huxley, and Denis Payton. They were dressed in casual clothes, in the middle of a dinner break. I was so nervous, but in an instant, they all stood up and each one came up to me and introduced himself, shook my hand, and said, "Hello, luv."

"May I ask a few questions?" I could barely swallow.

"Of course, luv. Sit down by me," Mike said.

I switched on my tape recorder, held up the microphone, and began asking him questions. Within minutes, the others had gathered around, leaned over Mike's shoulder, and talked into my microphone. My five minutes turned into thirty-five, and by the end I felt like I had really gotten some insight into each of their unique personalities.

As the DC5 ran down the stairs to the stage for the second show, Rick put his arm around my shoulder and said, "Let's watch this one together." It was one of those I-can't-believe-this-is all-happening moments. Rick and I remained friends for many years.

I didn't know it at the time, but I'd be spending much more time with the DC5 in the near future. That night was definitely a game changer.

My story on the DC5 appeared in *The Hornet*, the college newspaper. I thought my friends from school would think this was cool, but instead they criticized me for writing about a British "long-hair" band instead of a "serious" artist like Bob Dylan. I guess my colleagues felt the DC5 were too teenybopper. I didn't care.

One person who wasn't disappointed in my DC5 story was a girl named Tracy Thomas who lived in nearby Fullerton. She'd seen the article and told me how she and her mom published a weekly music newspaper (four mimeographed pages) called *Rhythm 'n' News.* It sold for five cents and was distributed to local record stores. Tracy wanted me to write for her. There was no pay, but I thought it would be fun.

While *Rhythm 'n' News* would sometimes cover popular groups like Herman's Hermits, they devoted more space to blues groups and Negro artists of the time. Often, my assignments were to cover performers like James Brown, Booker T and the MGs, Wilson Pickett, Tina Turner, Nina Simone, and Sam Cooke.

These performers mostly appeared at predominantly Negro clubs in South Los Angeles, a part of town many white people considered "unsafe." I was never afraid, though some of my friends were shocked that I would go out on these assignments. The clubs were small and not as well-known as the Hollywood Palladium or the Troubadour. But every time I would go for an interview, I was always treated well by the all-black audience and by the performers. While I stuck out with my blonde-haired, teenage-surfer-girl looks, the performers were happy to be getting some recognition via *Rhythm 'n' News,* and I was warmly received.

One of my first interviews was with James Brown. He had a hit with "Papa's Got a Brand New Bag," was known then as "Mr. Dynamite," and would soon go on to become the "King of Soul." He asked me to meet him in his room at the Continental Hotel on the Sunset Strip. He was as kind and sweet as he could be, and I tried not to be distracted by his hairdresser, who was setting his hair in huge rollers to help get the kink out for the bouffant hairdo he wore at the time. James was one of the few stars I asked to autograph a picture, and I'm so glad I did.

My assignment to do a story on the Beach Boys led to my first meeting with Derek Taylor. He'd been the press officer for the Beatles, but had left the Fab Four, moved his family from London to Hollywood, and set up his own public relations firm. He did publicity for the Beach Boys, the Byrds, most of the groups on Dick Clark's Caravan of Stars, and a few others.

I scheduled my Beach Boys interview through Derek's office, and, as I always did, I took Derek a copy of the article and introduced myself in person. We had a long chat in his office on the Sunset Strip, and he began to contact me whenever he wanted to publicize one of his acts. I saw a lot of him in late 1965. Very early on, I realized how important it was to make solid connections to gain *entree* to the stars of the day.

I'd gone on a few assignments with another writer at *Rhythm 'n' News*, and one day she said, "I'd really like to go to work for *Tiger Beat* and get paid for doing these stories."

"What's *Tiger Beat*?" I asked. She showed me a copy, and I agreed: It *would* be great to get paid for all the interviews I'd been doing. I bought a *Tiger Beat* at the grocery store and, flipping through it, noticed that Derek Taylor wrote a monthly column called "Group Scoops."

The next time I was at Derek's office, I told him I thought it would be so cool to work for *Tiger Beat* and asked him to arrange an introduction. He grabbed the phone and called Ralph Benner, editorial director of *Tiger Beat*, and told him a little about me. Then he held his hand over the receiver. "Can you go over for an interview with Ralph at 4 p.m.?"

"Of course," I answered.

Since I had never expected anything to happen so quickly, I had no resume, no copies of my work, nothing. But I had on a nice dress. After a quick "thank you" hug, I left Derek and drove over to 1800 Highland Avenue in Hollywood, about five miles away. I arrived at 4 p.m., sharp.

The receptionist was a cute gal with bright red hair and tons of freckles. I was distracted by the wall behind her desk, which was covered with big, black-and-white photos of rock stars: Cher, sticking her tongue out at the camera; Peter "Herman" Noone making a funny face; Mick Jagger in action on stage.

That receptionist was Laudy Powell, and I'd find out shortly that she was also a *Tiger Beat* staff writer who'd cofounded the magazine along with Ralph and publisher Chuck Laufer. All three had worked for *Teen* magazine and had left to start *Tiger Beat* in September 1965. Chuck bought the use of Lloyd Thaxton's name to boost the magazine's profile; Thaxton was the host of a daily, nationally televised teen dance show, and his name on the cover lent the new magazine some credibility.

But *Tiger Beat* was an almost immediate success and, by October 1966, Thaxton's name was dropped.

Laudy, who'd once been featured on the cover of *Teen* after winning their "freckles" contest, was ten years older than I, more mature, and married. She was somewhat reserved when we first met; I don't think she even knew why I was there.

Ralph was in his early thirties and put me at ease with his relaxed, down-to-earth personality. He asked me about my writing, what I'd been doing for *Rhythm 'n' News*, and my future plans; I told him I was about to finish junior college, planned to get my bachelor's degree in journalism from San Jose State College, and really wanted to work for *Tiger Beat*. Ralph asked me to rewrite two of my articles in *Tiger Beat* style and bring them back to him.

I stayed up late, yanking out a lot of "who-what-where-when-why" and replacing it with *Tiger Beat*-style stuff about what my subjects looked like, acted like, and smelled like. I forgot about sounding like a professional journalist and wrote more like a teenaged girl who cared about cute dimples and shiny hair. I found it easy to do.

Ralph seemed surprised to see me back in his office on Monday and amused that I wanted to wait around while he read my stories on the Dave Clark Five and James Brown.

"I think we can use these," he said as I held my breath. "How would you like to start working part-time in January?"

I couldn't believe his offer. I'd expected the occasional freelance assignment. Instead, we came up with a five-day-a-week work schedule, right on the spot.

Last week, I hadn't even heard of *Tiger Beat*; this week, I was working there—and receiving college credit for it, too, thanks to an arrangement with one of my professors.

I admit that I laughed when I saw my first *Tiger Beat* article. Ralph tweaked the Dave Clark Five story I'd auditioned with and published it in the March 1966 issue. He'd headlined it "The Dashing, Daring Deeds of The Dave Clark Five" and added things about the group like, "Incidentally, their feet are cute." I had mentioned in my story that the guys were often barefoot, and Ralph gave it that teen-scene spin so crucial to the magazine's young voice. That was my first lesson in what *Tiger Beat* readers were after.

After I finished junior college, Ralph asked me to come to work full-time. Five days a week, I drove up to Hollywood and went out on assignments I was given, each of which I considered a blessing and a privilege.

At the time, I had no idea of what lay ahead for me.

Chapter 2

Flying High with Jefferson Airplane and the Stones

A half-year ago, I had been a college freshman attending mixer dances and worrying about passing my English Lit final. Today, I was flying off to San Francisco on the spur of the moment—without any luggage or even a change of clothing—with a soon-to-be-legendary rock band. And my parents and my boss were cheering me on.

I realized early on that the traditional writing techniques, Associated Press style and ethics guidelines I was learning in journalism school weren't going to be of much use to me as a *Tiger Beat* writer. Ralph explained right away that *Tiger Beat* readers didn't want to know about their idol's sexcapades, and they didn't give a hoot if they wrote their own songs. I was told to focus on things teenaged and pre-teen girls could relate to: Mick's favorite color or what Paul liked to eat for lunch. We turned our attention to a pop star's thoughts on girls with short hair or why they always wore a particular strand of love beads. You wouldn't find us writing about Davy's new girlfriend; everyone was presented as single and free and looking for just the right girl, one who liked sunshine and home-baked cookies and thought the color green was just groovy! We didn't mention that Rob was slutty and favored girls with big bosoms; instead, we wrote about how he liked "all kinds of girls, especially sweet-natured ones who love walking on the beach like he does!" Exclamation points were as important as the signed pin-ups of our featured stars. I swore sometimes that Ralph counted the number of exclamations in each issue.

We *TB* writers had our own lingo, of course. A teen idol was a "fave," short for "favorite," a photo was a "pic," and two or more of them were "pix." "Love" was spelled "luv" and "laugh" was "laff." Pretty much every fave from the Monkees on signed his full-color pin-up (which were a *Tiger Beat* staple, of course) "Peace and Love." Guys were "heavenly" or "outasite," and if they were "cool," they were "gear." We had stock headlines, like "Why He's Special" and "Telling Tales on..." All our headlines were typically more titillating than the stories they slugged. A piece titled "Bobby Rushed to Hospital!" would likely be about how a fave drove really fast to get to Cedars Sinai when he heard his sister had broken her ankle and was in the ER. "Pete's Truest Sorrow" might turn out to be, by the second paragraph, about how sad the Herman's Hermits singer was when his twelve-year-old cocker spaniel died peacefully in her sleep.

We were there to offer mostly innocent, subliminally sexy copy that an eleven-year-old in Akron could dig, as the saying went.

By June of 1966, I'd been at *Tiger Beat* for six months as a part-time editorial assistant and had gotten the hang of the jargon and the less-than-naughty angle on most every story. In that time, I'd also wrapped up a second year of j-school at Fullerton Junior College. Just three credits shy of my Associate of Arts degree, I'd been accepted to the journalism school at California State College at San Jose, then the best journalism school in the state. I made plans to live in the dorm at Cal State San Jose in the fall, but the summer of 1966 messed up that plan in what *Tiger Beat* would have called "a really groovy way!"

Back in February, I'd met Skip, a cute boy who was in a band from British Columbia, at the Whisky A Go Go on Sunset Boulevard. The Whisky was already legendary, the club where all the bands wanted to play. A gig at the Whisky was a real triumph for any up-and-coming rock act, and it was the first place to feature that strangest of Sixties trends: mini-skirted girls dancing in cages hanging from the ceiling. Skip was friends with the Jefferson Airplane, and while Skip's band was in town recording, I joined them at the Whisky to see the Paul Butterfield Blues Band perform. That night, I met the Airplane: singer Signe Anderson, singer/guitarists Paul Kantner and Marty Balin, guitarist Jorma Kaukonen, and bassist Jack Casady. They were huge in the Bay Area, where they'd had a couple of hits, and whenever they came down to LA we'd get together, usually at the recording studio or at clubs to see other bands perform.

By 1967, Grace Slick had replaced Signe as lead singer, and the band went on to have hits with "White Rabbit" and "Somebody to Love." Eventually, they were inducted into the Rock and Roll Hall of Fame. When we first met, however, they weren't well known in Southern California.

The day after the Paul Butterfield show, Skip was given the official Ann Moses tour of Southern California, ending with dinner at the wharf in Huntington Beach. On our way home to my parents' place in Anaheim, Skip and I were driving down Brookhurst Avenue when a car pulled up next to us and the four boys in the car starting throwing paper cups at us and screaming, "Faggot, queer, get the hell out of here!" at Skip. I knew this was how some guys with long hair were treated at the time, but I'd never experienced it and I was petrified. They continued to follow us, holler at us, and harass us. I was especially afraid they would try to run us off the road—I was driving my parents' car! We were both terrified, and Skip ended up staying the night in my brother's bedroom.

The Airplane returned to LA the following month, and Spencer Dryden was now their drummer. They invited me to their all-day recording session. They had to catch a plane back to San Francisco that night, and I offered to drive them to the airport. As we pulled into LAX, Spencer and Paul asked, "Why don't you come with us?"

"I only have my camera and purse," I laughed. "How can I go to San Francisco?"

"We'll get you what you need," Spencer said.

"And you can stay with us," Paul added. They shared a San Francisco flat. I thought to myself as I parked in short-term parking, *Why not?*

Once inside the airport, I used a pay phone to call Ralph and tell him I was headed to San Francisco and wouldn't be in for a couple of days. He was thrilled—he and Chuck were always trying to get me to "hang" with rockers. In fact, Chuck used to say to me, "Why are you coming into the office so early? I know you're out at clubs late at night. Just come in when you want." He and Ralph both wanted me "out there" at recording sessions, on TV show sets, and at Hollywood nightclubs getting as much face time as possible with faves. They knew this would make my articles more personal and real, that I'd get the inside scoop on all the stars if I was out and about. I was happy to oblige.

In those days, air travel was more relaxed. You just walked onto a plane and, if there was an empty seat, you took it. At some point during the flight, a stewardess would come take your airfare—in this case, $25 for a round trip from LA to San Francisco.

After we landed, we headed to the guys' flat, only minutes from Haight-Ashbury, the epicenter of hippie culture. They gave me a quick tour: antique velvet couches, rock concert posters from the Fillmore Auditorium, and a lot of those then-popular melted Coke bottles, which were warped, stretched and twisted into how they'd look if you were tripping on LSD.

We settled in the living room, and Spencer said, "Let's get high!"

I figured I'd be honest with my new friends. "I've never done that before," I confessed. They told me how great it was, and that I should definitely try it. As we passed a joint around, they guided me in taking a deep puff and holding it in my lungs as long as possible. I did a lot of coughing and sputtering. They suggested I take smaller "tokes," and that seemed to go a little better.

After about fifteen minutes, they were both glassy-eyed and asked me, "How do you feel?"

"I don't feel anything," I said. So much for trying drugs for the first time.

We headed off to the Cow Palace. On the drive there, they told me we were going to a Rolling Stones concert, and that Jefferson Airplane was one of the opening acts. "How groovy!" I replied, trying to appear nonchalant. Inside, I was screaming, "Oh my God, oh my God, oh my God!"

At the arena, the guards let us right through—there were no large, laminated backstage passes on lanyards back then. You were on the list, or you weren't.

After the Airplane's set, we hung around backstage while Sopwith Camel played. The Stones arrived—in a pair of long, black Cadillacs, because they were already huge stars—and immediately ducked into their dressing rooms. Once they'd heard that Joan Baez was there, all five Stones were gathered around her.

Mick spotted me standing in a corner and came over. "Hello, luv!" We chatted for several minutes about the movie *Charlie Is My Darling,* the first documentary film about the Stones, shot during their two-day tour of Ireland in September. I tried to keep my voice calm, which wasn't easy standing this close to Mick Jagger with his slim body, long hair, and pouty lips. I could not believe how casually he treated me, no star-trip at all. Meantime, I was thinking, *My god, Mick Jagger is chatting me up when he could be over there, talking to Joan Baez!*

Before long, Brian Jones, Bill Wyman, Keith Richards, and Charlie Watts walked over, nervously lit cigarettes, and joined in our conversation. They wanted to know about growing up in southern California and told me all about their upcoming holiday in Hawaii. I couldn't take my eyes off Brian's gorgeous suit of shiny black fabric with wide white stripes. I later showed a picture of it to my mom and had her copy the top half for me. It was one of my all-time favorite jackets.

After the Stones took the stage, I placed myself just below Mick's feet at center stage—so close that during the show I was showered with Mick Jagger sweat—and began madly shooting pictures. My Nikon didn't have an auto winder or any automatic settings, so it was just me and my light meter battling the stage lights surrounding Mick and the guys while also trying to enjoy their show.

These turned out to be some of the best pictures I ever shot—dramatic, high-speed black-and-white photos of Mick dancing, his arms held high as he played the tambourine—and were used to illustrate an October *Tiger Beat* story about the Stones by Derek Taylor, and in the November issue under the title "My Surprise Visit with the Stones."

We got back to Paul and Spencer's late, and we went through the same pot-smoking routine as before: passing a joint, me coughing, and then...nothing. No buzz, no munchies, no giggles. I was both super keyed up and exhausted by the emotional experience of hanging out with the Rolling Stones.

It might have been the era of "free love," but when I slept with Spencer that night, he didn't lay a hand on me. So many of these rock-and-roll guys treated me respectfully, more like a kid sister than a potential conquest. Then again, there was no shortage of young girls hanging around who wanted to bang their fave.

After breakfast at a little café in Haight-Ashbury and a visit to a couple of head shops—another first— I booked a flight home. First, though, I had to see "the Haight." It was the soon-to-be-history-making hotbed of hippie culture, and we wandered from shop to shop, where Zig Zag rolling papers, concert posters, love beads, and incense were sold. That was one hell of a twenty-four-hour adventure!

Chapter 3

Getting My Kicks: On the Road with Paul Revere and the Raiders

In early 1966, I was assigned to cover Paul Revere and the Raiders pretty much exclusively. They were huge in *Tiger Beat* at that time, and I got to know them well as good friends as I followed them all over Los Angeles. I was a regular on the set of the weekday national musical variety show *Where the Action Is*, which they hosted. I love some of my memories of that time: lead singer Mark Lindsay, dressed in a fake fur caveman suit, "dragging" me by my hair at the Los Angeles Zoo; me on a motorbike, holding tight to Jim "Harpo" Valley's waist; and just how genuinely nice to me this group of pop superstars really was.

Originally an instrumental band out of Boise, Idaho, Paul Revere and the Raiders were founded in the late fifties by organist Paul Revere Dick. As the Downbeats, Paul, singer Mark Lindsay, and drummer Mike "Smitty" Smith played teen dances all over the Northwest. They changed their name to Paul Revere and the Raiders in 1960, and had a hit with an instrumental, "Like Long Hair" the following year. In 1965, bass guitarist Mike

"Doc" Holliday was replaced by Phil Volk, nicknamed "Fang" because of his protruding front teeth. Doris Day's son, record producer Terry Melcher, wanted to work with the group, so they relocated to Los Angeles, where they, with new guitarist Jim Valley, were signed by Dick Clark Productions as the house band on *Where the Action Is.*

That summer, I arranged to follow the band and their opening act, Dino, Desi & Billy (Dino Martin, Desi Arnaz, Jr., and Billy Hinsche), on several concert dates in Maryland and Florida. I was expected to fly home after the last Florida date in Miami, because Gloria Stavers, editor of our biggest competitor, *16* magazine, wanted to photograph both groups in Miami, and she didn't want me around while she was there.

At the time, *16* was the biggest teen magazine in the country. It had begun publishing in 1957, so we at *Tiger Beat* were the new kids on the block with just a year under our belt. Gloria and her staff hated that we had created quite a stir in that year's time, because we were based in Hollywood and were in constant contact with all the celebrities. Based in New York, *16* mostly printed stock publicity photos of faves, while we ran personal "I was there" and "my day hanging out with" stories. Our candid photos sometimes featured Laudy or me in the shot with the musicians and TV stars we covered. We also ran full-color, full-page glossy "pin ups" in our magazine, while 16 ran mostly two-color process photos on newsprint. Frankly, these pix looked cheap, and fans weren't fooled. I had plenty of complaints about Ralph and Chuck over the years, but I have to hand it to them: They spared no expense in creating a better, and therefore more competitive, teen magazine. Gloria, stuck way over on the other side of the country and working with smaller production budgets, hated the edge we had on her publication. And, therefore, she appeared to hate all of us at *Tiger Beat*.

No problem. I had four exclusive days on the tour bus with the guys before Gloria would turn up in Miami for what would likely be a couple hours of photos and a handful of quick interviews.

I arrived in Baltimore to find the hotel mobbed by more than 300 screaming young girls. After the show that night, Harpo and Fang insisted I had to be "initiated" to be on a Raiders tour, by which they meant I had to go with them to their room to get high.

"You know, I tried pot twice with Paul and Spencer from Jefferson Airplane," I explained, "and it didn't work. I didn't feel anything."

They suggested I give it another try, and they would "prove" to me that I was stoned. We sat in a little circle on the floor and passed around a joint. I remembered how I had coughed and choked the last time, so I took small puffs and held my breath as long as I could. After a few minutes, I was feeling a little different—a little mellow, a little giggly. That's when Harpo and Fang went into action. They changed out of their stage costumes—the blue velvet military waistcoats, black knee-high boots and three-corner hats they wore on stage as part of their Raiders gimmick—and began to crack me up by impersonating first an elderly couple grocery shopping, then a hippie chick with the munchies who was eating everything in sight. It rarely occurred to me, back then, that I was living the dreams of the girls I was writing for: Hanging out with cute teen idol rock stars until the wee hours, having the very kind of chaste fun I was forced to write about.

Well, mostly chaste. In a *Tiger Beat* story about that night, I would have left out the part about passing a joint with these groovy young faves. Also the part about how we stayed up until 3 a.m., after which Harpo escorted me back to my hotel room and put the moves on me.

We were interrupted by a knock on the door. I peeked; it was the front desk clerk. "No gentlemen are allowed in a single room!" he barked at me. To which Harpo responded, "I was just saying good night" as he made his hasty—and disappointed—exit.

The next morning, I joined the guys again. Mark and I had breakfast together, during which Harpo and Fang cracked me up by making silly faces and jabs about our secret "initiation" of the night before. Once we had landed in Jacksonville, I got to work, talking with Dino, Desi, and Billy, and taking pictures of the Raiders and singer Tommy Roe, who was also on the tour.

Laudy and I were always writing about how teen idols

loved meeting and talking to their fans, but that wasn't necessarily the case. I'm sorry to say there were plenty of teen idols who were too busy, or too self-absorbed and snotty, to spend much time seeking out fans. On this tour, I discovered that the Raiders were the rare exception: These guys actually got up at the crack of dawn to accept long distance, collect calls from teenaged girls calling from some little town in Kansas or wherever. Jim and Mark and their band mates spent hours each morning talking to these love-struck strangers. They really were, as we might have said in *Tiger Beat*, "the grooviest to their fans!"

Back on the bus, Mark inflated an air mattress and climbed up into the luggage rack above the seats (yes, he fit!) and slept until we stopped for lunch. Paul and I hunkered down with my tape recorder, and he told me the entire history of the Raiders. Tommy Roe and Smitty both played their guitars pretty much continually, and there were sing-a-longs with all the guys. Talk about being in the right place at the right time—wow. I was overwhelmed to be a part of this incredible group of musicians.

In Tampa, I took a call from Derek Taylor's office. They were wondering if I'd gotten the stories and photos I wanted. I explained I was still working on separate interviews and photo sessions. It seems Gloria Stavers had decided to arrive in Tampa following that concert, rather than in Miami as had been planned. She had sent a message to the boys' tour manager: "Get that girl from *Tiger Beat* to stay away from the boys for the next three days," because Miss Stavers was on her way to Florida and it was "her turn."

I was furious at this cheap power play. Paul was upset, too, and tried to make peace with a promise of a secret, two-hour photo shoot with the Raiders before their afternoon concert in Orlando.

Things got worse when Gloria turned up as we all were boarding the bus for Orlando. She got right in my face and hissed, "I'm taking over now, so I had better not see your camera out of its bag or you'll be off this tour bus!"

I didn't know how to respond. I was nineteen; Gloria was forty. My mom was forty-seven, so Gloria's words felt like a tongue-lashing from a critical parent. Was I intimidated? You bet I was. I made my way to the back of the bus and pretended to catch up on my sleep, as many of the guys did each day. But after I collected myself, I got angry.

Okay, bitch, I thought. *I was going to be a pleasant professional. But you just fucked with the wrong sunny California girl.*

By the time we arrived in Orlando, I had a plan. I hadn't gotten where I was by being timid, so there was no way I was going to cave in to her nasty threats. And I knew I could count on my friends to help me.

I'd already gotten some great photos before Gloria stomped onto the scene, and because I knew when her photographer would be shooting the Raiders (Gloria didn't seem at all interested in Dino, Desi and Billy), I managed to turn up wherever she wasn't. Harpo called my room one morning and said, "Come on over! I'm shaving, and you can take pictures!" Mark phoned and said, "Hey, there are fans outside my room. You can grab a shot of them getting autographs." Dino, Desi, and Billy found a secluded spot by some wonderful palm trees, and I got group and individual portraits. In the boys' hotel room, I shot Desi and Billy wearing Raiders uniforms. We had a grand conspiracy going on, and it was really a lot of fun to outsmart Gloria.

Looking back now, I get it. Gloria was twice my age and smart enough to see that having cute young girls as editors and writers meant she was working at a deficit. Readers were more likely to relate to Laudy's story about how much fun she'd had at Cher's wardrobe fitting or to photos of me having lunch with Jack Wild than they would to a story by someone their mom's age gushing about the cleft in Sonny Bono's chin. Likewise, the young, horny boys we were writing about were more keen on hanging out with reporters their own age than with a contemporary of their moms. *Tiger Beat*'s Los Angeles proximity to stars, coupled with the fact that Gloria's was no longer the only teen fan magazine on the stand, had to have troubled her.

Still. She didn't have to be such a giant bitch to me, either.

After the show, we headed for Miami, and again I sat quietly in the back of the bus, made notes, and observed the camaraderie I later chronicled in my two-part story about being on tour with these bands. Gloria watched Desi and me fighting, like a couple of teenaged friends, over the only pillow on the bus; she noticed that when we arrived in Miami, some of the guys asked me to walk with them on the beach; she noticed that I was included in the shenanigans of dodging the teen girls who lingered in the hotel hallways. Whatever the reason, Miss Stavers left the tour that night.

After the Florida shows, the guys all boarded a plane headed for their next gig in Louisville, Kentucky, and I stopped off on the set of *Flipper*, a TV sitcom about a problem-solving dolphin set in Miami. I interviewed Luke Halpin, one of the cute teen stars of the show, then flew back to Hollywood, where I knew I'd be seeing the Raiders again in just a few days.

My next tour with the Raiders would be just as much fun—although maybe not quite as innocent as this one had been.

Chapter 4

Pix and Pin-Ups and Fun Fax on Faves: The Business of Tiger Beat

When the first issue of *Lloyd Thaxton's Tiger Beat* debuted in September of 1965, the cover price was thirty-five cents and a one-year subscription cost $3.50. The advertisements in the first issue ranged from Halsion pimple cream to weight loss "tabules." There were ads selling photos of the stars from "Jeri of Hollywood" and 8mm movies of the Beatles from something called "Beatle Buys."

But the stand-out ad, the one that ultimately tells the tale of *Tiger Beat*'s success, was a "book" that was in fact a five-inch-by-eight-inch, sixteen-page booklet, no doubt written by a *Tiger Beat* staffer, titled *Beauty and Popularity Secrets.* It sold for a dollar, and when I say it sold, I mean it *sold.* This little number, which would be republished over and over again over the years, attributed to different "authors" (most popularly as *Susan Dey's Boys, Beauty, and Popularity*) every few years, was the beginning of the marketing success of many such products created and sold through *Tiger Beat* over the years.

Before he became publisher of *Tiger Beat,* Chuck Laufer taught English, journalism, and history in Southern California high schools. He launched *Coaster* magazine, later renamed *Teen,* in 1955. In 1957, Chuck sold *Teen,* but stayed on as editor until he, Ralph Benner, and Laudy Powell left to start *Tiger Beat.*

He got the idea for *Tiger Beat* after publishing an independent, one-shot magazine crammed with Beatles photos. The way he told it, this little one-off sold 750,000 copies in two days. Chuck wanted to compete with *16* magazine, which at the time was the only teen publication focused on cute boy celebrities.

From the very first issue, Chuck's angle was that *Tiger Beat* stories would be more authentic because they'd be based on first-person interviews conducted right there in Hollywood. So, each issue featured stories like "I Met the Stars of *Peyton Place*!" by sixteen-year-old Sandi Demming. While the magazine's mascot was a cute little cartoon tiger, Sandi was the spirit of *Tiger Beat*: a teenaged girl who was thrilled to be hanging out with cute superstars.

The thing about Sandi Demming was, she didn't exist. "She" was Ralph, or sometimes Laudy, writing in the voice of an excited teen. He figured stories about cute boys would be more credible if they came from a teenaged girl, rather than an editorial director in his thirties. The concept of a young woman writing firsthand about her experiences "among the stars" played an important role in my own *Tiger Beat* story.

Issue Two featured ads for another in-house product, *Tiger's (Private) Address Book!* This was a booklet that touted "over 100 home addresses of your favorite celebs!" In Issue Three, Laudy's "Meow" column debuted, with pictures of twenty-eight-year-old Laudy posing alongside Chad and Jeremy and Carole Shelyne, "the girl with the glasses" who was a popular dancer on *Shindig*.

These early issues also featured stories about the female music and TV stars of the day, but it wasn't long before the editors realized that cute boys got the biggest response from readers. Chuck and his staff were still trying to find a groove, so the first couple of issues included a lot of filler articles, like a cartoon feature called "The Beatles Visit *Peyton Place* A Go Go," "Teenage Misfits! How Not to Be One!" and "The Big Cat Predicts," where the magazine's mascot looked into his crystal ball and announced contrived and mostly made-up things like "Mark Lindsay will fall in love...hard!" or "Bob Dylan won't be as influential." (Boy, did he get that one wrong.)

By the February 1966 issue, back issues of *Tiger Beat* were offered for fifty cents per copy. One of the two "trial" articles I had submitted to Ralph before they hired me as editorial assistant ran in this issue, too: the opening story titled "The Dashing Daring Deeds of the Dave Clark 5, Like Wow!" The story included a photo of me interviewing Mike Smith at the Melodyland Theater some months before. I wish I had my original copy of the article, because Ralph's rewrite made some substantial changes.

Here's Ralph's rewrite of my lede paragraph: "There was a whirling all around me. Here I was...at last...staring straight into the eyes of Dave Clark and sitting close enough to Mike and Denny that all I'd have to do was reach out and touch them. The room was dark and filled with excitement. I'd waited and hoped so long for this moment that I wasn't quite myself...What girl would be!"

I'd been excited to meet the DC5. But I hadn't been delirious.

My paid, working internship began in January, and my title was editorial assistant. After I came on board as a staff member, the fictional Sandi Demming was relegated to her new role as president of the Save Our Stars Club. My second trial article appeared in the April issue: the interview I'd done with James Brown the summer before. But the minute I started my internship in January, I was accepting assignments from Ralph, who sent me to visit the set of *Where the Action Is*. I'd met the Raiders when they'd visited the *Tiger Beat* offices a few months before, but during each new assignment, I reacted like what I was—a teenaged girl from Anaheim who couldn't believe this was happening to her.

I also had a lot of genuine fun as I gained experience. I conducted interviews with the Raiders between shots on the TV set, or accompanied them when they filmed on location at places like the Los Angeles Zoo. Being around the Raiders was always like play time, and yet I'd always come back to the office with lots of great material for upcoming stories.

There was never a time when I wasn't out on assignment or back in the office writing my stories. And, oh, how I loved writing those stories. I had learned to type in high school typing class, and my parents bought me a manual typewriter when I graduated so I could type my college papers. But when I went to work at *Tiger Beat,* I worked on that most amazing of things: an IBM Selectric electric typewriter. I was already a fast typist, but with the electric typewriter, I could write as fast as the thoughts popped into my head.

By the May issue, I was contributing information for Laudy's "Meow" column, although she'd write it as if it were she who'd been hanging out with the Dave Clark Five or whomever. Laudy's column was still being touted as "The never-before-told stories about your favorites from the gal who PERSONALLY knows them all!" In reality, Laudy—an excellent writer who contributed many articles to *Tiger Beat*—rarely left the office. When she did, it was only for an occasional photo op with a celebrity to illustrate a "Meow" item.

At this point, I was averaging at least one by-line per issue. I'd travel to LAX at 4 a.m. to spend a one-hour layover interviewing Herman's Hermits, or I'd visit the set of the popular soap opera *Never Too Young* to interview cute British cast member David Watson. I also wrote articles with no byline, where "*Tiger Beat*" visited someone like Burt Ward (who played Robin on *Batman*) at home. At this point, I imagine my bosses didn't want to invest too heavily in promoting me until I'd proven myself. I didn't take it personally—I was too busy flitting from one assignment to the next, excited and appreciative for each and every one. Each day was a new adventure.

Early on, when I was working as a *Tiger Beat* reporter, my articles were edited and marked for typesetting by art director Norbert Jobst. When the copy came back from the printer (all the way from Chicago!), Norbert would paste down the title type, mark the black and white photographs with crop marks for the printer, then place the photos into the layout. I didn't see the blueline—the final copy of the finished magazine—before it was given the go-ahead for printing. Just like our readers, I saw my finished articles for the first time when we received the printed copies at the office, just before they hit newsstands. I was as thrilled as the readers when I saw my work come to life in this way.

After Chuck and company became more invested in me, my assignments became more exciting. Touring with the Raiders, taking my first plane ride, hanging out with the Who—I couldn't get enough of my new work life. I was glad I'd chosen excitement and adventure over finishing my journalism degree at San Jose State. But, truthfully, I was learning so much at *Tiger Beat*, it was almost like being in j-school. My photography skills improved every time I did a celebrity photo shoot; I learned about magazine publishing, marketing, and public relations. I learned the art of networking, which is at the heart of how Hollywood operates, and which served me well in various other parts of my life later on.

When I was promoted to feature editor in July 1966, I left my job at Disneyland, where I was still working weekends and was the highest paid counter girl at $1.10 an hour. Chuck paid me $400 a month as *Tiger Beat* feature editor—the equivalent of $2.50 an hour. I thought it was a handsome salary. There were other perks, too: Ralph and Chuck told me to choose any car I wanted, and the company would lease it for me, gas and insurance included. I chose a gold Pontiac LeMans with air conditioning and power everything. I even had a $25 a month expense account. As Sandi Demming might have said, "I couldn't believe all of this was happening to me!"

Chuck really liked the idea of a fresh-faced, Southern California girl as the "face" of *Tiger Beat*, and I was that girl. The gimmick of showing me as a gal-on-the-street was a solid one, but it was more than a gimmick. I really did all that work! The October 1966 issue, in which I was officially introduced as the feature editor, included a three-page spread of photos I'd taken of the Rolling Stones in San Francisco, in addition to the writing I'd done, bylined and otherwise, for that issue. Including me in the photographs made it plain that *Tiger Beat* really was right there, rubbing elbows with the stars we wrote about.

It was a pretty fair trade—or at least I thought so at the time. I had the flashy job, the company car, the expense account. And Chuck had the income from selling photographs I had taken, without sharing any of the profits with me. In that same issue where I was announced as feature editor, we began offering 8 x10 photos, "Exclusive to *Tiger Beat* Readers." About half of these photos were ones I had taken. They could be yours for only a dollar apiece, unless you wanted to pay an extra 25 cents for "rush handling."

I still laugh every time I hear that phrase. What readers didn't know was, there was no such thing as "rush handling." Nothing was sent out from *Tiger Beat* until we had a total of 200 orders, the minimum number of pieces the postal service would mail at the cheaper bulk rate—another prime example of Chuck's marketing savvy. Photos taken by me and staff photographer Kenny Lieu continued to be sold for a dollar apiece for the next five years. As far as I know, Kenny never shared in any of the proceeds from these sales, either.

Still, I was making money and having a great time. Little by little, I was allowed to make other contributions to the magazine. I don't remember if it was my idea to feature a "guest editor" on the contents page, but it *was* my idea to have the guest editor—Raider Mark Lindsay was our first—hand-write his message to readers. Guest editors didn't really work on that issue, but this popular gimmick further established our proximity to stars and gave us still more "insider" credibility with readers.

Chuck really hit his promotional stride in mid-1966. After watching an industry screening of *The Monkees* pilot, he secured rights to exclusive publishing deals on this brand-new TV show and its stars. He licensed a deal for a monthly *Monkee Spectacular* magazine, as well as for products like "Monkee Love Beads" and "Monkeeshades" sunglasses. Eventually, Chuck made product deals where he controlled everything from manufacturing to licensing. Our relationship with Screen Gems, which held most of the Monkees copyrights, meant I had exclusive access to the group. Chuck repeated such business relationships often over the next decade or more—the old you-scratch-my-back-I'll-scratch-yours ploy, writ large with dollar signs. The magazine benefited from our exclusive access to stars, and the record labels and TV studios benefited from our constant promotion of their product.

So, Chuck would send Davy Jones on an all-expenses-paid vacation to the Bahamas, with our photographer Bob Custer tagging along. The amazing vacation photos, especially those of Davy in his swim trunks in the crystal-clear water of the Bahamas, made for a fabulous *Tiger Beat* spread. From there, Davy traveled to England to visit relatives, and Bob got some amazing shots of Davy on a horse, holding his elderly father's hand. Davy got a free vacation, and we got priceless coverage for our readers.

As the magazine grew, so did our ad revenue. In full-page ads, we plugged groovy mail order operations like "Carnaby Square," which sold mod caps, mini skirts, go-go boots, and granny glasses. In September of 1967 we ran full-page color ads from shoe store chain Thom McAn, showcasing their "Monkee Mini Boots" for $5.99; by mid-1969, we were running full-page ads from record labels, a company selling a "new flash cube-cartridge camera," and Bardahl auto racing gear. While I wasn't privy to the financial goings-on at *Tiger Beat,* I did realize the owners made more money from ad sales and the sales of their in-house products than from the newsstand sales or subscriptions.

Many of the ads were for our own products, especially those staple-bound booklets we marketed as "books." One, *The True Story of Paul Revere and the Raiders,* was written by me and filled with photographs I'd taken during the week I was on tour with the band. I was paid a flat fee of $100 to write this "book," which didn't have my byline on it. There was one that did, however: a little number called *Secrets by Ann Moses.* I have no memory at all of what this book was about, but you can bet my "secrets" were things like "Cilla Black used to bite her nails, until she figured out that dipping her fingers in hot chili sauce would cure her of this gross habit!" Hey, it was *Tiger Beat,* and it was the Sixties.

Of course, both of these ads carried Chuck's moneymaking tagline: "Add 25 cents for rush handling!"

The Monkees dominated the pages of *TB* for about two years, and therefore, so did the merchandizing of the Monkees. In the November 1967 issue, the inside front cover was a full-page, four-color advertisement for Monkees paint by numbers sets, available at all leading chain stores. Right around this time, Chuck also increased the number of in-house products we sold, like *The Monkees '67 Concerts Photo Album* and a three-foot-wide Monkeeland Giant Illustrated Wall Map ("Your Friends Will Freak Out When They See This on Your Wall!" our full-page ad promised). Chuck commissioned Frank Morton, an excellent portrait artist, to create fine-art line drawings of each of the Monkees that sold for $1 apiece. Four more of those booklets were also available: *Pow! Here's Peter Tork, Marvelous Mike Nesmith! The Dynamic Davy Jones!* and *Mighty Micky Dolenz.*

Was Chuck taking advantage of our teen and pre-teen audience? I never looked at it that way. Back when I was a fan of James Darren, I would have done extra chores to earn extra cash for a book about James.

One of my favorite independent ads was for something called the "Living Necklace," sold by a company in New Jersey. The necklace had a *live* rainbow fish swimming and playing inside a glass bubble pendant. "The fish will live and grow!" the ad proclaimed. Included with your $3.88 purchase was a free "Color Wand" that changed the color of the water to match your clothing. I wonder if these poor fish lived as long as Sea Monkeys did.

In the January 1967 issue of *Tiger Beat*, Chuck upped the ante, pulling way ahead of *16*, which was printed on cheaper newsprint. We'd always had a slick color cover and back page, but now Chuck added ten glossy color full-page pin-ups of our most popular faves. From that point on, I shot color as well as black and white film when I was out on assignment.

The success of those color pin-ups was the catalyst for our sister publication, which premiered in September 1967. *Tiger Beat's FaVe!* promised "20 pages of full color portraits of your favorite performers...and outasite picture stories with exclusive photos you won't see in any other publication."

By the early 1970s, this color-poster premium thing had really gone nuts. Included in the August 1971 issue was a giant color poster of David Cassidy, folded to fit into the center well of the eight-by-eleven-inch magazine. The following month, that same color centerfold was double-sided. One side was another giant photo of David; on the other, one-fourth of a wall-sized portrait of him. Readers had to buy the magazine for the next three months to complete their giant jigsaw puzzle, which could be stapled or taped together. We teased readers with a photo of me holding up the finished poster, which reached from my shoulder to my ankle—and I'm five-feet-two! If you happened to miss one of the four issues and needed to complete your room-sized poster, we sold each piece separately for $2. It was another genius Laufer marketing ploy, and we followed it with a wall-size poster of the Osmonds on one side and Bobby Sherman on the other.

In the meantime, my involvement with the magazine continued to grow. With the February 1967 issue, my "I Visit with the Monkees" column became a regular feature. In that same issue, Laudy handed over her "Meow" column to me.

"This is the last Meow column I'll be writing for *Tiger Beat*," she wrote, "and for a lovely reason. I'm now the proud mother of a baby girl named Andrea, and I just don't have time to run with groups like I used to. I'll still be the Associate Editor of *Tiger Beat,* but from now on my hours are strictly 9 to 5. Ann Moses will be taking over the column next month and I know she'll do an outasite job keeping you informed on what's happening."

With every issue, I became more and more involved in the actual production of *Tiger Beat*. Though my title hadn't changed, I was now responsible for story ideas and assignments (I couldn't write them all myself!). Chuck and Ralph sought my opinions at monthly editorial meetings, where we'd run through color slides and choose pin-ups and cover images. They came to rely on my input, which made me feel so much more a part of the team and important to the magazine.

I understood that our access to stars gave us an edge, and I was on a mission to make *Tiger Beat* number one by getting exclusive stories. I was the only reporter there when the Raiders took dozens of stuffed animals to a children's hospital—and I made sure we printed a handwritten note from Paul, explaining to fans why the band gave away the presents they'd sent.

Early on, I met Genie Franklin, better known as "Genie the Tailor, Seamstress to the Stars." We became fast friends, and she turned out to be a mentor to me. Genie was from New York City and was a few years older than I. She'd taken some acting classes in New York and was much more worldly than I. Whenever I spent time with Genie, I always learned something new, and whenever I was stuck for a solution to a problem I couldn't share with anyone else, Genie was there with a mature point of view and experienced advice.

When she proposed a kooky monthly fashion column for *Tiger Beat*, I asked her to write a sample installment, then took it to Ralph. He fell in love with her "magic genie" shtick. As well as a showcase for Genie, the column—about designing for and hanging out with her famous clients—was another scoop for *Tiger Beat*: The "seamstress to the stars" was one of our featured columnists, and crazy photos of Genie with her superstar clientele gave us even more edge.

I was happy Chuck let me really shape the look and feel of *Tiger Beat* during these years. No one ever told me to stay out of one aspect or another of the production. At one point, I insisted on cropping most of the photos myself, after I began to notice that our graphic artists often cropped half of a star's head out of the picture. The graphic artists didn't love my dabbling, but they tolerated it. I wanted *Tiger Beat* to look great.

As the magazine grew and we added more staff, like a second artist and more editorial assistants, I was free to pick and choose which stories I wanted to do. So, if I didn't care much about covering Sajid Khan—a much younger boy who starred in *Maya*, a TV show I didn't watch—I could pass the assignment along to one of my writers or an editorial assistant.

(Early on, I learned to give my freelance writers fake deadlines. Inevitably, they'd call me the day their story was due. "I'm almost finished! I'll have it to you in three days!" I was never late getting stories to the printer, because my fake deadlines were always set at least a week before I really needed the story. The writers never knew my trick—until now!)

I usually chose my assignments based not on whether they were the most fun, but whether my insights would enhance the finished piece. I might interview Mark Lindsay's housekeeper for details of his private life, because I knew what subjects Mark would rather I stayed away from when I wrote the piece. Or I'd grab the stories on the stars I'd become close to, like the Monkees, Dino, Desi, and Billy, and the Raiders, because I knew our rapport would improve the stories.

One of the columns I was proudest of, and one that I hung on to rather than assigning it to another writer, was the one "written" by Sally Field. Each installment was based on interviews I'd done with Sally on the set of *The Flying Nun*. She and I were the same age, and I could really relate to her, which I think was apparent in the writing. I loved our interviews and visits, and I still think fondly of Sally, who of course went on to enjoy a stellar movie career.

By the time I was officially named editor on my twenty-first birthday, I'd received a number of raises, a larger expense account, and a new leased car every year. I was making more money than my dad, a vice president of United California Bank, where he'd worked for twenty-five years. I had grown up in a middle-class household, and it didn't occur to me to spend my money on Beverly Hills hairdressers or shop for expensive clothes in fancy boutiques. Working for *Tiger Beat* was never about the money. I truly did it for the love of the work and the experiences.

Every once in a while, I'd get angry about some idiotic thing that had been said to me at the office, and I'd wind up looking through the *Los Angeles Times* classifieds the next morning. I'd tell myself, "I'd make a great secretary," but then I'd notice that secretaries were making about one-fourth of my monthly salary, and whatever had had me so shaken up was instantly forgotten.

One time I did drop in at Dick Clark's office. I'd worked with him on a show he produced called *Happening '68,* as well as with his office staff whenever I went on one of his "Caravan of Stars" tours. I thought, "It would be so much fun to work for Dick Clark. He's such a nice guy!" That was true, but when a friend who was one of his top employees told me her salary, I knew why Dick Clark was such a rich man. He paid his people peanuts.

There were times when, no matter how much I disliked something that was going to be published in *Tiger Beat*, I knew to keep my mouth shut. Like Chuck's brief "thing" for the Flying Cavarettas, a group of trapeze artists who appeared at Circus Circus in Las Vegas. He went often to Vegas and came back raving about this great-looking family. He was certain he could mold the four sisters and their brother into singers and teen idols. Right away, we were doing photo shoots and stories on the Flying Cavarettas. They never secured a recording contract—perhaps because none of them were singers—and were a total flop with our readers. But Chuck hung on for a while, and it was several months before they finally dropped out of the pages of *TB*.

In October 1969, Chuck launched his newest publication, *Rona Barrett's Hollywood*. Rona was a nationally known television entertainment reporter, and like *Tiger Beat's* early use of Lloyd Thaxton's name, Chuck contracted with Rona for the use of hers. She didn't actually contribute to the magazine, although she had approval of what went into each issue. Chuck hired a staff of editors, writers, graphic artists, and photographers to work solely on this magazine. My only contact with this project was my attendance at a gala launch party at the Beverly Hills Hotel, presided over by Rona and attended by numerous Hollywood stars including Mae West in a rare public appearance. Although I had nothing to do with this magazine, it would prove to be pivotal in my future relationship with Laufer Publishing Company.

Chuck, his brother and *TB* associate publisher Ira, and our new business manager Roland Hinz decided it was time to raise the cover price from thirty-five cents to fifty cents with the January 1970 issue. With each paid subscription, we now offered readers a choice of free gifts: Bobby Sherman's Love Beads, a *Tiger Beat* Love Charm Bracelet or Pendant Necklace, or a set of Bobby's Hearts and Flowers Stickers. Not long after that, we added David Cassidy's Choker Luv Beads to the free gift mix.

Tiger Beat and its sister publications were never about journalism. Chuck wasn't interested in the deeper meaning of a girl's love for someone she'd likely never meet. He didn't actually care how Bobby felt about his TV show being canceled or whether Donny was happy singing about puppy love. Chuck, like any good businessman, was looking at the bottom line. When he and Ira sold *Tiger Beat* in 1978—for a reported $15 million—its circulation was then 700,000 issues per month.

That's a heck of a lot of choker luv beads.

Chapter 5

Hanging Out with Lucille Ball and Dean Martin ...And Their Kids

Dino, Desi, and Billy were huge favorites of *Tiger Beat* readers. The trio was Dean Martin's son, Dino; Lucille Ball and Desi Arnaz's son, Desi Arnaz, Jr.; and their high school friend Billy Hinsche. In 1965, they had two Top Forty hits, "I'm a Fool" and "Not the Lovin' Kind," appeared on numerous TV shows, and toured as opening act with the Beach Boys, Paul Revere and the Raiders, The Lovin' Spoonful, and The Mamas and the Papas.

My very first *Tiger Beat* assignment was to go to Dean Martin's house and interview the boys for a feature titled, for some reason, "Shhhhh... 24 Hours with Dino, Desi & Billy." Dean's house sat at the top of Loma Vista Drive off of Sunset Boulevard, and when I pulled into the circular driveway, I felt like any other tourist taking a tour of the stars' homes. Except that I, awed by the beauty of this brick mansion and the perfect trees and gardens surrounding the property, had an invitation to go inside.

A few minutes after I got settled in a casual sitting room just inside the front door, Dean Martin, dressed in casual slacks and a V-neck cashmere sweater, strolled into the room. “Hi,” he said, stepping behind the mahogany bar. “Would you like a drink?” Since it was Dean Martin asking, I wasn’t sure he wasn’t offering me a martini.

“I’d love a Coke, thank you,” I answered sheepishly.

Dean was a huge Hollywood star. He headlined the weekly *Dean Martin Show* on TV, had decades of hit records, and had starred in dozens of movies, many of them with his former comedy partner, Jerry Lewis. I was surprised I was so dazzled by his good looks—he was as old as my father. I sat there, trembling like a rattlesnake.

Dean excused himself just as Dino, Desi, and Billy bounced into the room. From that first day, these boys and I were always casual and comfortable together. Dino and Billy were 15, Desi was 14, and I was 18. They treated me like a peer, and while Desi and Dino were certainly more mature after a life spent in the spotlight, they were also teenaged boys, fond of practical jokes and teasing one another. They were always a blast to be around.

After a brief tour of the ground floor, the four of us went upstairs to Dino’s bedroom. My room at home held a single bed, a dresser, a sliding-door closet, and a small bookshelf attached to the wall. Dino’s was the size of our family’s living room, with an arrangement of leather chairs, floor-to-ceiling bookshelves, television and hi-fi equipment, and the plushest carpeting I had ever set foot on.

The guys took turns telling about their day, from morning wake-up to their bedtime rituals. They teased each other throughout, and while Desi shot photos with Dino's camera, Dino grabbed my tape recorder and began to interview me. When I started taking photos, Dino pulled on a knee-length nightshirt, sent to him by a fan. We staged shots of Billy pouring a bucket of water over Dino as he slept, and the three of them having a pillow fight. Thinking ahead to my title, I took a shot of Desi with his finger up to his lips, making the "S-h-h-h" of the headline come to life.

This casual friendliness was repeated every time we four were together. Even though Dino and Desi were the children of famous people, they were sweet and unpretentious.

If I was nervous in Dean Martin's company, I was flabbergasted when I turned up for my next Dino, Desi, and Billy interview, held at Desi's mom's house on Roxbury Drive. Lucy herself answered the door.

She and Desi's dad, Desi Arnaz, Sr., had divorced in 1960. Lucy was married to stand-up comedian Gary Morton, and they lived in a very Hollywood Cape Cod-style mansion.

"Hi," I stammered. "I'm Ann Moses from *Tiger Beat* magazine."

"Come in, darling. The boys are expecting you." Lucy was warm and welcoming. Dressed casually in white capris and a sleeveless cotton blouse, she was wearing full make-up and red lipstick. She had her flaming red hair in a then-popular "bubble" cut and had bright red toenails peeking out of her sandals. I'd never seen anyone with a pedicure before.

Once again, I was standing this close to another *huge* Hollywood star. I'd seen every episode of *I Love Lucy* ever made. She was a legend, and there I was, taking a tour of the most beautiful home I had ever seen. She'd decorated it in Country French style, with the striking Mediterranean blues of the sea and yellows of the sun. Out back, there was a huge swimming pool, a pool house and cabana, and a performing stage that the boys used for rehearsals. Unlike some of the posh Beverly Hills homes I had visited, this was a comfortable family home. I just wanted to plop down onto the overstuffed sofas.

The guys arrived, and we settled in for several hours' worth of questions that would later be turned into stories like "10 Things You Never Knew About Billy" and the like. Later in the afternoon, Desi and I talked for hours for a "My Life by Desi" feature.

I'd get to know these sweet young guys a lot better a few months later, when I joined them on that Florida tour with the Raiders, and later still, when I traveled with them to Hawaii for two concerts with the Beach Boys and the Raiders in August 1967. Ralph and Chuck wanted photos of the two groups on the beach, in bathing suits, out boating, and dressed casually under swaying palm trees.

On that trip, I stayed at the famous pink Royal Hawaiian Hotel on Waikiki. It was great to be in Hawaii for the first time, but frustrating, too. The guys I was covering were all staying elsewhere and, in an age before cell phones, trying to communicate with them meant me swimming for ten minutes, then rushing back to my room on the twelfth floor to wait for the phone to ring, or checking with the front desk for messages. I wanted to enjoy the sun and fun of Hawaii, but I had a job to do.

I loved watching both groups perform. The Raiders and Dino, Desi & Billy took turns as opening acts, and that first night, after watching the Beach Boys perform, Desi took me out for a spin on the motorbike he'd rented. We took off as I grabbed tight around Desi's waist—no helmet, with my hair blowing wildly as Desi picked up speed. I'd never ridden on a motorbike before, and it was exhilarating and frightening at the same time. We flew past palm trees, the ocean crashing into the shore as we headed north along the beach—until we saw the flashing red lights and heard the blaring siren behind us.

I had never been stopped by a policeman, and I don't think Desi, who was 15 and had no driver's license, had been, either. I offered my California driver's license, and the police officer frowned and said, "You kids are out after curfew. If you head straight home, I'll let this go." I guess we could have played the kid-of-a-celebrity card, but we didn't.

The next day, I spent hours photographing both bands in the beautiful Hawaiian scenery. I got a lot of good shots, but many of my photographs didn't come out because the glare off the ocean made my manual Nikon settings all wrong in pictures I took too close to the water.

I was glad I never mentioned this to Dino, Desi & Billy's manager, Mack Gray, because he called not long after to ask me to shoot color photos for the picture sleeve of the group's new single, "My, What a Shame." We did the shoot on the set of *The Dean Martin Show*, with the boys in suits and ties. The record sleeve looked great, and I was very proud.

Dino, Desi & Billy hadn't had a hit in a while, but they still got a ton of fan mail, so we continued to feature them in every issue of *Tiger Beat*. When Desi became a regular on his mom's new show, *Here's Lucy*, he became even more popular. I arranged to interview Lucy for an as-told-to story about Desi, Jr.'s life, and it turned out to be one of the most memorable days of my life.

I met Lucy in her office at the former Desilu Studios, where her show was shot, and she was just as warm and as gorgeous in person as I remembered her. I lost all concept of time as I listened to one amazing story after another. I had arrived at 10 a.m. for our interview, and at around noon Lucy stopped.

"I'm starving!" she barked. "Join me for lunch?"

A man in a chef's coat brought in two plates mounded with a delicious-looking Cobb Salad, made famous in the thirties at the Brown Derby Restaurant at Hollywood and Vine. During lunch, Lucy surprised me by asking questions about my life. I told her about growing up in Anaheim, what an amazing seamstress my mother was, how my dad was a banker and my brother was in dental school. From her reaction, I think Lucy truly enjoyed hearing about my normal, middle-class life. I was touched that she would be interested.

Lucy gave me so much material, the article became a four-part series, illustrated with photographs that Lucy had copied for me. I'm sure she had no idea of the impact she'd had on me that day. She, a Hollywood legend, had treated me like I was a professional journalist from *Life* magazine. My day with Lucy remains one of my fondest memories. And there were plenty more to come.

Chapter 6

Catching That Train to Clarksville: Meeting the Monkees and Surviving Mike Nesmith

The first faves featured in *Tiger Beat* might have been Sonny and Cher, Herman's Hermits, and the Righteous Brothers, but the Monkees put our magazine on the map.

First introduced to our readers in the September 1966 issue, this made-to-order pop band had been assembled by television casting agents to cash in on the recent success of the Beatles, whose hit movie *A Hard Day's Night* was the inspiration for what became *The Monkees* TV show. Mike Nesmith was a failed folk singer; Micky Dolenz, the former child star of NBC's *Circus Boy* series; Peter Tork was a banjo and guitar playing folkie singer who had played in small Greenwich Village clubs, then made his way to California; and Davy Jones was a British actor who'd recently appeared on Broadway in the smash musical *Oliver!* Together, they were about to make television and pop music history.

The Monkees premiered on NBC on Monday, September 12, and I met the group for the first time the day before, on a press junket on the "Last Train to Clarksville"—actually a Union

Pacific Passenger Liner renamed for the occasion. The train left from LA's historic Union Station and arrived in the coastal town of Del Mar, which had been dubbed "Clarksville" for the day by the town's mayor. Once there, we headed to an outdoor performance space where a warm-up band entertained the crowd. After a while, we heard the roar of four helicopters flying overhead. They landed on the beach, and out of each helicopter jumped a Monkee, dressed in the long-sleeved, doubled-breasted shirts that became their signature look. These four young guys ran for the stage, where they performed their soon-to-be-Number One hit, "Last Train to Clarksville," which was already moving up the Billboard charts by then. The audience went wild, and I remember thinking, *These guys are going to be huge!*

After the performance, we all piled back onto the train, the Monkees in tow. They played two songs live in the caboose. (Both on stage and on the train, the guys played their own instruments.) During the rest of the two-hour ride, they visited with fans and with us in the press car. I noticed as I chatted with each of the guys that they stayed very much in character: Mike was sardonic, Peter sweet and dimwitted, Davy the cute, girl-crazy Brit with the sexy accent, and Micky the joker.

(He wasn't joking when he asked for my phone number, though. I'm not sure what I would have done on a date with Micky Dolenz, but I never got to find out. He never called.)

Although the Monkees' show had yet to debut, Chuck had already inked that deal with Screen Gems for promotional and merchandising access to the group. That meant I had to get myself over to *The Monkees* set at Screen Gems Studios, only a few miles from the *Tiger Beat* office, and get that initial interview.

I admit it. I was nervous. This was my first time on a Hollywood television set. The Monkees worked on a closed set, meaning no one was allowed on the soundstage without special permission. The set itself was a huge warehouse with lights hanging from the ceiling, big black cables snaking across the floor, and all sorts of stagehands, makeup artists, actors, and extras milling around.

As I timidly walked onto the set, I spotted Davy sitting in a director's chair with his name stenciled on the back (each of the guys had one of these). He waved me over, put his hands on my arms and kissed me gently on the cheek. I felt immediately welcomed and let out a deep sigh of relief.

The guys were on a break from shooting, so Davy gave me a tour of the set before he was called away to film a scene. He introduced me to the hairdressers and the makeup artists, and to Jim Frawley, the director, who explained that when the bell rang, it meant "all quiet on the set." I watched in fascination as they shot and reshot the same scene, each time from a different angle: a wide view, a close-up of the actor speaking the lines, the view from behind the actor showing the response from whomever he was talking to, and sometimes close-ups of individual reactions. I'd never realized how time-consuming it was to get one minute of footage on film. And because this was the Monkees, there was lots of improvisation going on all the time. Over and over again, I heard the assistant director yell, "Quiet on the set!" before the person with the clapperboard (that little chalkboard slate that lists the producer, scene number, take number, director, camera, and date) would hold it up to the camera. The cameraman rolled film, the board clapped together, and the director yelled "Action!" Over and over again, I also heard the director yell, "Cut!" if an actor made a mistake or their improvisations went too far. Then they'd start the whole scene over again.

I spent a lot of time on the *Monkees* set and in their dressing rooms over the next two years, and I never knew what to expect when I opened that stage door. Davy might be in a prince costume, Mike in Western clothing, Peter in an Indian headdress, or Micky in a trench coat and curly wig.

In January of 1967, my "I Visit the Monkees" column premiered. Each month, in pictures and captions, I told a story about the groovy on-set fun of filming *The Monkees*. We always included a picture of me with one of the Monkees in each column, to validate *Tiger Beat's* insider status: me riding on a bike with Davy on Screen Gems' New York street set; me helping the make-up artist comb Peter's hair; me posing with the Monkeemobile. That car was a lot more friendly to me than

Mike Nesmith ever was, let me tell you.

That first visit, I did what I could to get reacquainted with Peter, Davy, Mike, and Micky. They were all cordial, but it would take many more visits to the set before they would really be comfortable opening up to me—most of them, anyway.

Of all the Monkees, I think I got to know Peter the best. Before being cast as a Monkee, Peter had lived as a true hippie. Active in the peace movement during the "love-in" days of the late 1960s, he was a folk singer with a lot of friends in the music business. He was also much smarter than his television counterpart. He was well-read and liked to study different religions.

Peter was always kind to me, and we had many wonderful conversations besides the interviews he knew would wind up in print. He was always after me to drop acid with him—I think it was his way of drawing me into his inner circle of friends. I had smoked pot, but I kept hearing about "bad trips" people had had on LSD.

"I'm just too afraid of what might happen," I kept telling Peter. And he always assured me, "Don't worry, I'll be there with you. I promise you'll have a good trip." He was sincere and persistent. But I was too chicken.

If Peter was the quietest and most introspective of the four, Micky was the most comical and fun. He had the biggest need for attention, and you just wanted to be around him constantly. Although he never sought me out, and we didn't truly become friends, Micky was cooperative and professional. Whether I was there for interviews, photos, or just to watch the guys shoot the TV show, he was always friendly and made my job easier.

I also wasn't among Davy's inner circle of friends, but he always greeted me warmly and treated me as a colleague. I've always thought the reason he was the most popular Monkee—something our readers made clear in their fan mail—was because he was the most genuine. He never acted "the star," and appeared to love those he worked with—the make-up artists, the director, even the extras on the show. He was living the dream.

The same can't be said of Mike Nesmith. Maybe you've seen the video of the Monkees auditions, where Mike's sardonic and smart-alecky personality is on full display. That's the real Mike. From the start, as I visited the *Monkees* set almost daily, Mike always made it clear he thought my questions were silly, a waste of time, and beneath his intellectual level. He didn't care that it was my job to get to know the Monkees as individuals, to find out things *TB* readers wanted to know, including silly things like "What's your favorite color?"

Mike wanted the cover of *Rolling Stone*, but it was *Tiger Beat*'s teenybopper readers who watched his TV show, bought the Monkees' records, and asked their parents to take them to a Monkees concert. The readers were my focus, so I kept after Mike until I got what I needed.

My first Mike story was that old *Tiger Beat* "story of my life" chestnut. He kept interrupting my interview to say he couldn't understand why anyone would want to read about his life. I had to ask at least five questions to get even one response from Mike, but I persisted and got my story.

Later, he'd find other things to do during our interviews: change costumes, make phone calls or sandwiches, or—most memorably—pin cigarette packages to his dressing room wall. Often his response was, "That's the most blatantly stupid question I've ever heard!"

I persevered. And, where Mike was concerned, I often failed. The climax came on the *Monkees* set in October of 1967. I'd been following Mike around all morning, unruffled despite his rude comments and taunting remarks. Finally, he turned to me and said, "Look, I'm twenty-five years old. I have a wife, a child, and another on the way. I don't have time for your teenybopper shit. But I tell you what. If you fuck me, I'll do the interview."

I didn't take Mike's "deal" seriously. I figured he was just pushing my buttons, and so I walked out of his dressing room and back to the set. Mike didn't speak to me again for nearly a year.

During that time, I was able to get "Mike stories" thanks to his lovely wife, Phyllis, who was willing to meet with me often for interviews that became articles about her husband in *TB*.

And we needed all the coverage we could get on the Monkees, as we geared up to launch a new, all-Monkees magazine called *Tiger Beat's Official Monkee Spectacular* in

April 1967. After that, hanging out with these guys became my main assignment. As features editor of *Monkee Spectacular*, I spent most of my workdays at the indoor Screen Gems set or at Burbank's Columbia Ranch, where they filmed outdoor scenes.

Because we also debuted a third Laufer publication called *FaVE!* in August of that year, we really needed to stretch for story ideas. In production meetings, we'd weave an entire two-page article from a one-sentence interview quote. From my on-set interviews with each of the Monkees, I could get "Davy's Life Story!" or "Peter's Life Story!" There were always articles like "Davy's Life as Told by His Father" or his sister, and "Mike's College Days as Told by His Teacher." We got permission to contact the boys' families, and even secured exclusive rights to all their baby pictures (always a reader favorite).

Sometimes it was obvious we were stretching for story ideas. In the July 1967 *Tiger Beat*, we even ran a piece titled "Micky's Mother Interviews Ann Moses." (I'd spent the day with Micky's family, and while we were setting the table for dinner, Micky's mom said, "Hey, let me interview you!") After a while, we published articles on Micky's sister Coco, too, and she began writing a series of articles for the magazine. Anything with a Monkees angle, no matter how far-fetched, was gold.

In January of 1967, I joined the Monkees at a concert in San Francisco. We'd devoted a lot of pages to debunking the rumors that the four couldn't play their own instruments, so I was thrilled to cover a live performance for the magazine. We flew up on their chartered jet, and I rode to the Cow Palace in Davy's limo. *Tiger Beat* sent our photographer, Bob Custer, and he and I watched the show from beneath the stage.

I'd seen them play at their promo appearance, watched them lip-sync on the TV show, and had been to their recording sessions. But I wasn't prepared to see them live before 20,000 screaming fans. I was awestruck at how exciting and professional they were as live performers. I'd seen the Beatles at the Hollywood Bowl and the Stones at the Cow Palace, and this Monkees performance was right up there with those two.

One of the things that truly set the Monkees' performances apart was the light show and the slides projected on a big screen behind them—both relatively new ideas in live music shows. Peter Tork and Bob Rafelson, one of the TV show's producers, were inspired by similar tricks they'd seen at the Fillmore in San Francisco. The Monkees added political statements to their concert slide show by including images of civil rights marches—they were among the first to do so.

By this point, I'd begun contributing freelance articles to *New Musical Express*, a popular British weekly newspaper—more on that a little later—and was the go-to person when British faves wanted to meet the Monkees. I'd call the producer's secretary, Marilyn Schlossberg, and she'd leave my guests' names with the gate guards at Screen Gems. When Jimmy Page and the Yardbirds came to perform in LA, they called me to take them out to meet the Monkees. Likewise, Dave Clark and his group, during one of their umpteen visits to LA. Dave spent the entire day on the set, and I got some great photos of the meeting and an exclusive story out of it.

Not long after the Cow Palace show, the Monkees kicked off their 1967 tour of America and the UK with a Hollywood Bowl performance for 17,000 fans. Backstage, as they were getting into their stage costumes, Micky whispered in my ear. "At the end of our last number, '(I'm Not Your) Steppin' Stone,' I'm going to jump into the pool in front of the stage." I alerted our photographer, and when the moment came, he was ready and caught the incredible shot, just as Micky hit the water—a spectacular end to a spectacular show.

After they completed the European leg of their tour, I joined the guys in Dallas to do the rounds with them before a concert there. I rode with Peter in his limo to an appearance on a local TV station, and we were mobbed by fans, who crawled onto the hood of the car and beat on the windows and roof. After the television taping, they escaped the same group of fans by running the half-block across the roof of the building and making a mad dash for the limos. It could easily have been a scene from one of their TV shows, but it was real.

I joined the Monkees for dinner before their show at the Sam Houston Coliseum. Davy had heard of a British restaurant a block from our hotel, so he gathered everyone for an authentic English meal. Mike was the only Monkee who didn't join us; he took a group of his relatives to dinner elsewhere, instead.

At the Red Lion Restaurant, Davy encouraged everyone to order steak, kidney, and mushroom pie with Yorkshire pudding. I'm pretty sure I stuck with a slab of prime rib with my Yorkshire pudding. As we waited for our meals, Peter and Davy carried on for fifteen minutes, acting out various British accents. Really fun!

One of my fondest memories of this time was witnessing Davy's kindness toward his friend Jan Berry, whom Davy invited to the Monkees concert in Houston. Jan had been half of the duo Jan and Dean, who, next to the Beach Boys, had been the biggest act in surf music in the early Sixties, with hits like "Surf City," "The Little Old Lady from Pasadena," and "Dead Man's Curve." In April of the year before, Jan had been in an automobile accident that nearly killed him. He survived but was left with severe brain damage. Unable to walk or speak, he was completely paralyzed on his right side. Publicists told the world that he'd be fine, but he wasn't. Jan and Dean were finished.

I was dumbstruck when I first saw Jan walk in unsteadily and take a seat. He spoke like a five-year-old, drawing with crayons on paper, then proudly showed off his pictures, which everyone praised. At one point, he told me privately, "I know my ABCs," then proceeded to slowly recite the letters of the alphabet. It was heartbreaking to see this former idol in this condition, but also really lovely to watch how everyone treated him with great respect.

I was touched by Davy's tenderness, but not surprised. I already knew about the time he'd taken a plane from LA to Phoenix to visit eleven-year-old Rhonda Cook in the hospital. Rhonda had been hit by a car on her birthday and had had her left leg amputated. She had been carrying a Monkees album when the car hit her, and word got to Davy about her accident. He asked that the press stay away, but the story wound up in *Tiger Beat* and in *The Arizona Republic*, anyway.

The Monkees were the hottest thing in music and on television, outselling the Beatles and the Rolling Stones combined in 1967. They played to sold-out arenas. And then, a little less than two years after they burst onto the scene, their television show was canceled and their records stopped selling. In my September 1968 "Meow" column, I quoted Micky as saying, "I'm not particularly distressed at the ending of our TV series as it stood...we ended it ourselves...we wanted the show to be different each week. It was a question of format." The show had run for fifty-eight episodes, the last of them airing on March 25, 1968. The band went on to make the movie *Head*, which was a commercial disaster.

As we did with every teen idol, *Tiger Beat* began slowly phasing out our Monkees coverage. It's just how the business worked. My "I Visit the Monkees" column morphed into "I Visit the Stars." We continued to include articles like "The Monkees Tour Japan and Australia" but mostly as photo essays. By the December 1968 issue, a photo story on the making of *Head* was the only mention of the Monkees. Davy continued to appear on the covers for a few months, but we were already amping up for the latest hottie: a pop singer named Bobby Sherman. In the March 1969 issue, we announced that Peter had quit the band.

Not long after that, I got a call from Peter. He was working on putting a new group together, and asked if I'd do a "Tour of Peter's New House" type story, just to keep his name in print. I knew *Tiger Beat* readers wanted to know what was next for each of the Monkees, so I drove out to Peter's new place in Studio City, where he greeted me at the front door, stark naked. He cordially invited me in, and as I walked through the house, I realized I was the only person with clothing on. He said, "Our house is clothing optional, so you're welcome to take your clothes off if you like."

I think I muttered, "I'm fine." Never an especially modest person, I still couldn't have taken a tour of my friend's house without my clothes on. I was working! I kept my eyes on the house, and when I encountered Peter's friends, I looked into their eyes as we spoke.

I was glad I hadn't brought my camera that day.

Mike Nesmith had also recently taken me by surprise—although not by getting naked. Ten months after Mike propositioned me and stopped speaking to me, I was visiting Columbia Ranch for that photo story about their movie *Head*. During a break in filming, Mike asked to have lunch with me.

While he sipped hot brandies—four of them, as I recall—Mike confessed that his months of rude behavior had been an attempt to get me angry enough to write a story with some "guts." Most pop stars at the time told me great tales of debauchery that always ended with "But, hey, don't print that!" They didn't want to be photographed smoking cigarettes or quoted talking about their steady girlfriend back home, if they had one. But this interview with Mike was different: He wanted me to write about him as something other than a manufactured teen idol.

For the first time, Mike talked to me on a personal level. He told me he wanted me to become a better writer, by writing about deeper, more important things, after which we talked about his jeep, his new tape recorder, the girl modeling clothes at the restaurant, my boyfriend, and his future after the Monkees. Deeper, more important things.

I got a great essay out of this meeting, which I published in the May 1968 *New Musical Express* under the headline "Mike Nesmith Wanted Me to Expose How Rude He Was." But by then, *Tiger Beat* readers weren't interested in Mike's new tape recorder or in Peter Tork's skinny-dipping pool parties. The Monkees were in eclipse, and *Tiger Beat* had already moved on to the next teenybopper superstar.

Chapter 7

More Monkee Shines

It's hard to imagine, in a world where celebrities are given practically live coverage, that teen star gossip in the late 1960s and early 1970s came to fans via their mailboxes—and only once a month, too. Rather than sensationalize the drug-fueled sexcapades of some of the stars, it was our job at *Tiger Beat*, *FaVE!*, and *Monkee Spectacular* to downplay all that for our mostly pre-teen audience.

Tiger Beat readers were rabid to know every detail of their faves' personal lives, especially their love lives. On the other hand, no ten-year-old girl wanted to read about how the boy she watched on TV every Tuesday night was a homosexual addicted to smoking banana peels. Fandom centered around a girl fantasizing David-Bobby-Donny as her boyfriend, a fantasy that could be disrupted by adult messes like jail records and pregnant girlfriends. Many of our readers were young, so these fantasies probably didn't involve sleeping with their fave, so sex wasn't even implied in our pages. We wrote about romance as if it involved a lot of hand-holding and the occasional kiss.

We knew readers liked intimate stories that fueled their

romantic-dinner-with-my-fave fantasies, so we wrote a lot about celebrity dating habits, and we focused on general ideas like what the guys looked for in the girl of their dreams or what they thought about going steady.

The goal of giving readers what they wanted was tempered by the business of promoting young superstars. We also had to consider that these young men (and women) had personal lives they wanted to protect, in some cases lives that didn't necessarily reflect the "image" their promoters and handlers wanted. We set the standard for this kind of balanced, make-believe coverage with the Monkees. The challenges of covering four horny young overnight sensations for three different pre-teen magazines was a crash course in what to say and what not to say in print.

At first, Mike Nesmith wanted no published pictures of his wife and new baby; later, we kept Davy Jones's marriage and baby a secret for many months. All of this was fine with us. In the world of teen faves, being married with kids was often lousy for a cute young idol's fan base, who wanted him single, sweet, and waiting to marry one of *them*.

When I first met the Monkees, Micky and Davy were single, Peter was dating Cass Elliot's younger sister, Leah Cohen, and Mike was married to Phyllis. During the first year of the group's superstardom, I worked overtime to sidestep real-life Monkee romances and sexual dalliances when I wrote about the group. It wasn't always easy.

For a while, Davy dated Sally Field, who was then starring in the Screen Gems series *The Flying Nun*. Were they dating for fun or publicity? I never had a chance to find out. Sally married her high school sweetheart in 1968, and we all breathed a sigh of relief—until Davy started being photographed with Dean Martin's daughter, Deana, after she did a guest appearance on the Monkees' TV show. They were, we feverishly reported, "just good friends!" Next up was British pop star Lulu, whom Davy met when she was the opening act for the Monkees in London. She dumped him when she found out he was living with Linda Haines, who was pregnant with his baby.

None of this, of course, made it into *Tiger Beat*. In my September 1968 "Meow" column, I mentioned that Davy had recently had dinner with Lulu and her boyfriend Maurice Gibb of the Bee Gees; the couple was back together after their public break-up in the spring of that year. Just as the press had honored Franklin Roosevelt's request to never photograph him using his leg braces, we stayed far away from the fact that Davy was living with his girlfriend. Because what was really important was that his favorite color was blue! And his favorite food was enchiladas.

Eventually, we had Davy and Linda's blessing to publish the story of their marriage of some nine or so months before and to acknowledge the birth of their daughter, Talia. By then, we had already tiptoed around another Monkee wedding when Micky married his girlfriend, Samantha, in July 1968. At the wedding, Sammy—a teen model and a regular on *Top of the Pops*—was several months pregnant.

Up until then, we'd been doing our usual captioning magic, tagging photos of the pair as "just friends who enjoy being together." These two were trickier, because unlike Davy, Micky never tried to hide his love affair. He and Sammy lived together in Laurel Canyon, and when I wrote about visiting Micky's house, I mentioned that Sammy had "helped him decorate."

By the time they married, the cat was out of the bag. In the December 1968 issue, we printed "A Thank You from Micky and Sam," thanking all the fans for their love and support of their union. Needless to say, we downplayed the very notion of heartbroken Micky fans who had planned to marry him themselves.

One of the last mentions of the couple was in my "Meow" column of February 1971: "Sad news from the Dolenz household: Micky and Samantha are on a trial separation. Seems Micky's lack of work and in-law problems are part of the difficulties. Adding an almost tragic footnote to the situation, their two-year-old daughter, Ami, had to be hospitalized in November after getting into some sleeping pills that were lying around the house. Ami's OK now, thank goodness." Even with a recent has-been like our Micky, fans didn't want to read about how he was hanging with the Hollywood party crowd, drinking and drugging and sleeping around, something he admitted to himself several years later. He and Sammy were divorced in 1975.

Occasionally, if he was cute enough, fans didn't seem to mind so much that their fantasy boyfriend was married in real life. Apparently, Mike Nesmith was cute enough, and readers who'd never had to deal with his personality continued to pledge their undying love for Mike. Fortunately for us, the married Monkee happened to be married to a lovely woman who—when her husband became more closed-off and full of himself—came to our rescue.

Mike used Phyllis as his "spokesperson," at least where *Tiger Beat* was concerned. In the August 1967 issue, we ran "The Girl Behind Mike Nesmith," with a great photo of Mike front and center and Phyllis' eyes peering from just behind his shoulder—an unfortunately accurate view of her place in his life. Rather than report on his philandering, the generic article related such fascinating details as the fact that Phyllis's closest friends called her April.

Sometimes, if you looked closely, you could find us tattling on faves. When Mike had a baby with one of his girlfriends in late 1968, while he was still married to Phyllis, Laudy was pissed. Never a fan of cheating husbands, she wrote a piece for *TB* titled "Christian Asks: 'Where's My Daddy?'" about how poor Phyllis was home alone with Christian and Jonathan, and Daddy was away all the time. Our readers didn't realize what the real story behind this was, but Laudy sure seemed to feel better after it was published. (Phyllis and Mike divorced in 1972.)

And what about Peter Tork? He might have been a free-love hippie, but from the get-go, Peter always seemed to be a one-woman man. Early on, we saw him often with Leah Cohen. He admitted to *TB* that they were dating, and borrowed from Micky with, "She's helping to decorate my new house." Leah wasn't threatening to fans; she wasn't rail-thin or a fancy dresser, and she looked more like someone you'd befriend, not someone you'd compete with for Peter's attention. Later, after leaving the Monkees, Peter was married for a few years to Reine Stewart, who had once been David Crosby's girlfriend, and they had a baby in 1970.

When Peter was seen getting off a plane in London with a young woman and a baby, I set the record straight in my *NME* column, but things were a little trickier at *Tiger Beat* when fans began writing to ask if he had been married and divorced. We ran a piece titled: "Now It Can Be Told: The Truth About Peter's Marriage." He went into great detail about falling in love at first sight with Jody Babb, whom he had divorced in 1960. In true *Tiger Beat* fashion, Peter looked back upon that time as "a learning experience" that had "made him a better person."

We were in the business of making dreams, not crushing them.

Chapter 8

Goin' Places I've Never Been: On the Road with the Raiders and the Standells

When I wrote in my "Meow" column that my upcoming trip was a "New Year's present from *Tiger Beat*," I wasn't kidding. Ralph and Chuck were so pleased with the pile of photos and interviews from my August 1966 trip, which we'd turned into many different stories and layouts, that they wanted me to travel with the Raiders again for an eight-day tour of some of the southern states.

Chuck was a shrewd businessman. He knew the eight-by-ten glossy prints of my photographs from the last Raiders tour were selling like crazy, and he wanted to keep up the pace with new inventory. So, off I went, on tour with the Raiders again.

This time, the tour included several of the regular acts from *Where the Action Is*: the Guilloteens, the Robbs, Ian Whitcomb, Keith Allison, and the Standells. In addition to snapping new photos of all these acts, I would do new interviews that we could turn into dozens of upcoming features.

In early November, I flew into Columbus, Georgia, where I met the Standells: Dick Dodd, Tony Valentino, Larry Tamblyn, and John Fleck. I was immediately drawn to Dick, the lead singer and drummer for the band. He was, as I described him in my first *Tiger Beat* article on the group, so "un-Hollywood." Tall and slender, he had warm brown eyes and irresistible dimples when he smiled. I didn't realize that he had such beautiful brown skin because his mother was Mexican. I only knew I couldn't keep my eyes off him.

We sat together a lot on the tour bus that week. It wasn't crazy love, but it was definitely a major crush. On our third night, there was a knock on my door. I was hoping it would be Dick, but instead, it was his cocky band mate, Tony Valentino. I was dressed in my baby doll PJs, but I invited him in, naively thinking he just wanted to talk. We hadn't spent any time together, so what else could he want? I didn't know Tony considered himself the Casanova of the group.

I grabbed a note pad and pen, sat on my bed, and began writing notes in longhand. I figured we were doing an interview, but Tony had something else in mind. Before I knew what was happening, he'd unzipped his pants, pulled out a couple of inches of his penis, which wasn't even fully erect, climbed onto the bed, and tried to pull aside my pajama bottoms. "What the hell are you doing?" I hollered, and pushed him away before he could actually touch me.

He looked surprised. "I thought we'd just have some fun."

I told him to find some "fun" somewhere else and pushed him out the door. I was horrified.

I continued to rave about Dick in letters to my parents, written on Holiday Inn stationery: "Dick was a Mouseketeer when he was nine, ten, and eleven years old," I gushed, referring to his regular slot on *The Mickey Mouse Club*, which had been the most popular kiddie show on TV in the Fifties. "So I've been bugging him constantly, asking him questions about those days. Poor baby."

Because I knew he'd tap-danced on *The Mickey Mouse Club*, I taught Dick a tap dance routine to the song "Meet Me in St. Louis" that I had learned and performed as a child. We tap-danced for the other guys for about an hour. By the time he had to go on stage, he was really worn out.

For the first time ever, I realized I wanted to do more than tap-dance. On the fourth night of the tour, I got a knock on my door, and this time it was Dick standing there. He took my hand, led me over to the bed, and we sat next to each other, kissing and then kissing some more. My heart was racing, and I could tell his was, too. But he was quite the gentleman, and before he left my room, he kissed me one more time. I peeked through a crack in the door, watching him as he headed back to his room, skipping down the hall. Then he broke into a self-congratulatory high kick of his heels—first on his left, then once more on his right. I've never received a more touching compliment.

There were other fun moments on this tour, all of which I recorded in various *Tiger Beat* features. In San Antonio, the Raiders visited a children's hospital where they sang a cappella for the sick kids there, which was a real treat for me. At the concert that night, President Lyndon Johnson's daughter, Lynda Bird Johnson, was in the audience—along with her four secret service agents, of course.

After the show, Dick rode with me to the airport, kissed me good-bye, and promised he'd call once the tour was done. As I flew home on the plane, I made a mental checklist for the next few weeks:

1. Find a gynecologist and get on birth control.
2. Find an apartment in Hollywood and move out of my parents' house.
3. Hope and pray that Dick calls as he promised.

I was still a virgin, but my infatuation with Dick had convinced me it was time to change that. I knew the basics about how to go about it, but not much more. When I was about thirteen, my mom had called me into the kitchen and, as she tore up pieces of lettuce for a salad, she ran through the mechanics of sexual intercourse. Once Mom was done with the basics, she wrapped things up in a surprisingly open-minded fashion for someone born in the 1920s. Instead of telling me I should never, ever have sex until I was married, she said, "Making love is something you do with someone you care for." I took her words to heart.

Birth control was a snap. My friend Genie the Tailor recommended her OBGYN in Beverly Hills, whose name was unfortunately Dr. Blood. He was an excellent doctor and prescribed the pills I needed to help me into womanhood safely.

I chose the third apartment I looked at—a one-bedroom, furnished, with its own carport—just in time for Dick to return from his tour. We saw one another several times a week, hanging out at the clubs on the Sunset Strip, going to movies, and walking on the beach for hours, just strolling along and talking.

By New Year's Eve 1966, we still hadn't slept together. We had a wonderful night out at the Whisky A Go Go on the Sunset Strip, watching the Turtles and Iron Butterfly perform, eating bar food and drinking sodas. In the backs of both our minds, I think, we were waiting to go back to my place.

After the Turtles' final number, we made our way to my apartment and were soon making out on the couch. Then we moved to the bedroom and were lying on the bed. Dick began to take off his shirt, and he gave me that look that said, "Join me."

Before long, we were both naked in the dark room; I was way too shy about my body to be comfortable with keeping the lights on. There wasn't much talking going on. There wasn't much passion going on, either. After a while, he just climbed on top and entered me. Was I ready for him? Not at all. Like many a young woman who looked up to rock stars, I thought sexual expertise was an automatic part of the rock-and-roll package. For the record, it definitely is not—at least, it wasn't on that night.

To say that losing my virginity was underwhelming would be an overstatement. Looking back, all I remember is that there were spots of blood on my sheets, and I was very sore after Dick left that night. He didn't spend the night. Maybe the whole thing was as disappointing for him as it was for me, but I can't tell you, because after that night he never called me again.

The funny thing is, I wasn't all that devastated. I sometimes wondered exactly where all the fun had gone, and why weren't we still hanging out together? But I didn't shed a tear. And if that was all there was to sex, I was pretty disinterested. A month later, I threw out my birth control pills. *Why bother?*

Chapter 9

Another Train: New Musical Express and "America Calling"

When I first saw the Beatles at the Hollywood Bowl in August of 1965, I had the same reaction I'd had when I saw the Dave Clark Five the month before: "I've got to meet those guys."

Not as easy a proposition as meeting the DC5 had turned out to be, but I tried.

I had a couple of contacts in Hollywood, as I'd begun writing articles for *Rhythm 'n' News* by this time. Derek Taylor had mentioned that the UK press corps were staying at the Beverly Wilshire Hotel in Beverly Hills, so the morning after that first Beatles concert, I drove up and talked to some of the journalists (all men, of course) who were enjoying the California sunshine out at the pool. I introduced myself to Chris Hutchings, a full-time reporter for the *New Musical Express*, one of the top weekly music newspapers in the UK. I grilled him about how I might go about interviewing the Beatles, and he just laughed.

No one just sat down and interviewed the Beatles, he told me. The band had rented a house up in Beverly Hills and had no plans to venture out during their week-long stay in Hollywood. I was pretty persistent, though, and he jotted down the phone number to the Beatles' rental house. I figured I was set. Chris also gave me tickets to that night's show. I'd get to see the Beatles all over again!

I must have called that number about fifty times before finally giving up. But Chris turned out to be a valuable contact in other ways. After I began working at *Tiger Beat,* I wrote to Chris early that year and asked him if he would find out if the *NME* editor would be interested in freelance articles from Hollywood. Many popular groups, from Motown to blues bands to groups only beginning to be popular in England, didn't get covered by *Tiger Beat,* but since I was seeing and hearing them anyway, I thought this might be a great outlet for some moonlighting.

By March, I had published a pair of articles in *NME*—one about the Beach Boys, another on James Brown. I was thrilled to be interviewing these artists and finally getting paid to write, besides. I stayed on with *NME,* and, after I went to work at *Tiger Beat,* I got permission from Chuck and Ralph to sell some of my *TB* stories to the UK market. My first reprint was published in February 1967: Mike Nesmith's "Life Story," told in his own words. I didn't get a byline, but for the next three weeks, *NME* ran Davy's, Micky's, and Peter's life stories in their own words, based upon my interviews with them.

NME sometimes also bought my photographs, and I made a nice bit of extra money. When I traveled to London in October

1967, *NME* editor Andy Gray invited me to lunch at a British pub. I was so in love with the Swingin' London scene by the time our lunch rolled around, my big plan was to ask Andy for a full-time job with *NME.* I thought it would be even cooler to live and work in London than in Hollywood, because London was the pop culture center of the world at that time.

Unfortunately, Andy told me there was no way he could arrange a work permit for me. But he had another offer: He wanted me to be *NME's* official Hollywood correspondent and write a weekly column, "America Calling," in addition to regular freelance articles that he'd assign. Ralph and Chuck agreed to let me work for *NME*, so long as my byline mentioned *Tiger Beat.* I was thrilled!

My first "America Calling" column appeared in the February 10, 1968 issue, with the headline "Bee Gees Meet Tommy Smothers and Our Ann in Hollywood."

The column also featured a "scoop" for them: I laid to rest that rumor that Peter Tork, seen getting off a plane in London with a young woman and her baby, was married and a new father.

Because I was in LA and had access to the people I wrote about, I was instantly a credible source when reporting for *NME.* Often, British bands coming over from the UK called to ask if I'd cover their Hollywood visit; other times, they wanted me to take them to Disneyland or get them good seats at a Little Richard show.

I was having the time of my life covering the faves of *Tiger Beat*, but I was also in my late teens and early twenties during this period and more interested in rock groups and folk singers we didn't cover. I loved when groups like Led Zeppelin, the Yardbirds, and Jethro Tull invited me to their Hollywood recording sessions, gave me backstage passes and front row seats to their concerts, or invited me to after-show parties.

One of the more memorable parties I attended was my first, thrown by Tommy Smothers for the folk singer Donovan, who was in town performing at the Hollywood Bowl. Tommy's guests included his brother Dick, Janis Joplin, Cass Elliot, Steven Stills, Graham Nash, Joni Mitchell, Michael Ochs and Michael's brother, Phil Ochs. And me! Tommy's house was a huge two-story affair, cantilevered over the edge of the Hollywood Hills above Sunset Boulevard. It was the first Hollywood house I'd seen with its own media room, where people kept sneaking off to smoke pot during the party. Donovan performed on top of the very high diving board over the swimming pool while guests danced and wandered around the pool, eating and drinking. After he finished his set, Donovan jumped into the pool, caftan and all.

Later in the evening, Phil Ochs, one of the better known "protest singers" of the day, won a door prize: a huge gift basket of wine, cheese, caviar, and fruit. He climbed to the top of the diving board and began yelling at the crowd of "beautiful people" about how disgusting it was that we were all partying while our soldiers were dying over in Vietnam. As a final gesture, he took his basket of bourgeois goodies and flung it into the center of the pool. Before his death in 1976, Phil wrote a song called "Basket in the Pool" about that night.

My job at *NME* gave me access to more than just parties. I spent a lot of time at the Troubadour, Doug Weston's famous nightclub, where most of the biggest folk acts got their starts. Bob Dylan did some of his first shows there in 1964; the Byrds met there during an open mic night the following year; and Buffalo Springfield played there the year after that. The Troubadour was small, seating only a couple hundred people, so every performance was an intimate experience with the artist.

I'd been going to the Troubadour since high school, and now I was on the guest list, covering performers like Hoyt Axton, the Nitty Gritty Dirt Band (with whom I became good friends), and James Taylor, whose debut at the Troubadour made me a lifelong fan.

In my *NME* stories, I could be more frank and tell "the rest of the story," unlike my *Tiger Beat* articles, which were written for a younger, more innocent audience. If I'd written about the Doors for *Tiger Beat*, I would have had to focus on Jim Morrison's dimples or John Densmore's super-shiny hair. In *NME*, I could stretch a little.

In a *NME* piece titled "Doors Forum Concert Fiasco," I reviewed their December 14, 1968 concert at the LA Forum, where they appeared before 14,000 fans. The show, I wrote, "was not only disappointing, but it was agonizing to watch 'Hell-child' Jim Morrison enjoy putting on the audience... The restless gathering was given 'Light My Fire,' only to have it drag on so long it was hardly recognizable. ...The climax of [Morrison's] egotistical put-on happened when he sat down, cross-legged, in front of the musically starved crowd and asked the audience what they really wanted? 'We can play music all night if that's what you want,' Jim said, 'but you don't *really* want that, do you? You want something different...' His mocking voice rang through the squirming crowd. ...The something different the audience then received was Jim Morrison reciting his own poetry. It might have worked in front of an intimate gathering of his friends, but the audience as a whole was more disgusted than appreciative."

I also noted that Jerry Lee Lewis, who opened the show, looked bored and played badly. In response to the endless booing, Lewis shouted out to the huge crowd, "I don't care if you all get heart attacks!" Lovely.

Even if *Tiger Beat* had been covering acts like the Doors and Jerry Lee Lewis, I wouldn't have been allowed to be critical or frank. The challenge of writing about Mark Lindsay's favorite color was finding a way to make it new and fresh, so it was great to be able to write about music I was into myself for *NME*, and to use some of the skills I'd learned in journalism school. I also got to meet and talk to musicians I might not have otherwise, like the Carpenters, Anne Murray, and Andy Williams.

NME wanted to run a piece on Williams in November of 1970, prior to his appearance on the *Royal Variety Performance*, an annual entertainment gala in the UK. I drove over to the NBC Studios, where *The Andy Williams Show* was shot, and Andy greeted me warmly and invited me to sit in the "living area" of his dressing room. He introduced me to his estranged wife, Claudine Longet, who was wearing a crocheted mini-skirt and a matching sleeveless blouse with a low V neck that accentuated her slim body.

My story covered Andy's role as producer of his TV show; how he felt about drug culture and the recent deaths of Janis Joplin and Jimi Hendrix; and his support of Bobby Kennedy, who'd recently been assassinated. What I didn't write about was how, right after barely shaking my hand, Claudine planted herself on Andy's lap and stayed there throughout our interview. That was weird enough, but she and Andy began making out, which continued as I asked Andy question after question. It was as if I wasn't in the room. I've never felt so awkward in my life.

I somehow maintained my composure, but I kept thinking, "What the heck is going on here?" The couple was separated at the time, but she was appearing that week on his show to promote her new record. Maybe she was trying to get attention so I'd mention her in my article, or maybe she craved the attention I was giving to Andy Williams. Who knows?

When I interviewed Anne Murray for *NME,* she'd just had her first hit with "Snowbird" and was in town to appear on Glen

Campbell's TV show. Anne was just two years older than I, so our interview was like chatting with a close friend. We sat on the bed in her hotel room for two hours, talking, and I could relate to how she felt about things—even when she talked about giving up her career for marriage. It's hard to believe in today's world, but back then, that's how we felt about being working women. For the past twenty years, I've played Anne's *Christmas Wishes* CD throughout the holiday season, and when I do, I always think of that nice afternoon we spent together.

I also play the Carpenters' Christmas album every year and feel so fortunate to have interviewed them for *NME*. Richard and Karen recorded some of my all-time favorite songs, but we gave them little attention in *TB*—they just weren't big with our readers. But readers in the UK were eager for news about them, so I met with the brother-sister duo at A&M Records, where Richard did most of the talking. Karen was shy, and seemed happier just listening to our conversation.

My first *NME* interview with the Jackson 5 took place at their new home in the San Fernando Valley when Michael was eleven years old. I'd met them once before when they first came to Los Angeles and the family was living in a townhouse that couldn't have had more than three bedrooms. *Tiger Beat* ran articles on the Jackson 5, and at that first interview, I remember being surprised because, as sweet as the boys were, I found them to be almost illiterate in their speech and in their writing. I asked them to fill out their "Lifelines," a popular question-and-answer sheet we published, always in a fave's own handwriting, in the magazine. I remember Michael wrote down one answer, and Marlon finished the rest for him. It was clear to me that these boys had spent less time in school than in working on their musical careers.

It paid off: When I met them for the *NME* interview a year later, the Jacksons lived in a huge house that overlooked the tree-covered hills of a compound protected with electric privacy gates. The property was beautifully landscaped and had dirt trails where the boys rode motorbikes.

I really regret not having my photo taken with the Jackson 5 at this early point in their career. Oh, how I would love to show my own sons a picture of me with Michael, before he became the King of Pop.

It became routine (though no less exciting) for me to be assigned by *NME* to cover British groups whenever they played in LA. One of my columns was titled "While in Los Angeles, Zeppelin at Garbo Hotel."

I already knew Led Zeppelin's Jimmy Page, because back when he was still a Yardbird, I'd arranged that visit to the Monkees set the year before. In early 1969, I met Jimmy and his new band at the Chateau Marmont, which I described as "the plush hotel where Greta Garbo, and more recently Mama Cass, once resided," even though it really was more shabby than "plush" during this period in its long Hollywood history.

The guys were rehearsing for a week of shows at the Whisky A Go Go, and when I arrived, they were strumming their guitars and singing—no amps, no drums. Led Zeppelin unplugged. Jimmy did most of the talking.

"America made us," he told me. "It takes two or three years to build up a reputation in England, but ... I didn't have any confidence in English audiences. The Yardbirds had their biggest success in America, and I just assumed it would be the same with us."

It was such a joy to be totally at ease with some of the biggest rock stars of our time, and to do serious interviews about the music. I tried not to be too blasé about any of it, although I did almost miss out on watching Elton John become an overnight success. I'd been invited to a press conference for Elton, but I hadn't heard of him before—pretty much no one had—and wasn't planning to go. I couldn't cover every new artist pitched my way. But a good friend encouraged me to attend Elton's opening night at The Troubadour, and I was glad I did. Quincy Jones, Gordon Lightfoot, Leon Russell, the Beach Boys' Mike Love and Brian Wilson, and Three Dog Night's Danny Hutton were in the audience that night. Neil Diamond introduced Elton, and all of us there were shocked and amazed by Elton's performance.

The next day, I headed to Elton's press conference with a whole new attitude. However, it was a fiasco. Uni, Elton's American record label, held the conference in a dark Universal

City screening room. Elton and his group were seated, but could barely be seen, and for some reason the journalists weren't given a press mike, so we couldn't hear one another's questions.

In addition to the Hollywood music press, UNI had chosen to invite high school and college newspaper reporters who asked silly questions. The scene was embarrassing, although Elton seemed unfazed and answered each question quite seriously. We couldn't even get a photo of him because the lighting in the room was so dim. I never did have a one-on-one interview with Elton John.

Another British superstar I didn't have a chance to interview was Lulu. But by the time I reviewed her 1968 American debut at the Coconut Grove in Beverly Hills, I'd already had an unpleasant run-in with her in my personal life. (More on that later.) Was it coincidence that my *NME* review, titled "Lulu Blasts British Boys," was kind of snarky? I wrote, "The crowd overlooked her music hall costume and enjoyed the lively set of tunes she chose, her No. 1 hit 'To Sir with Love' being a favorite." I noted that her "date" for the after party was Davy Jones, using quote marks because Lulu's dates with Davy were always for show—and this time, I knew, designed to make her famous boyfriend back home jealous.

I mentioned how, during a guest appearance on *The Joey Bishop Show*, Lulu had said, "I much prefer dating American boys. They're much more courteous. In England, the boys expect you to call them for dates and then go 'round and pick them up, too!"

I figured the boys back in Britain wouldn't love reading that. Hey. I wasn't a news journalist. I was a woman scorned.

My most prolific period at *NME* found me writing about one of my top personal faves: Elvis Presley. I first wrote about The King in 1968, when I covered his famous television comeback special. Elvis never appeared in the UK or Europe, but his diehard fans there were hungry for any updates. I was only too happy to be the one to satisfy their needs. I wrote about his first live appearance in 1969 at the International Hotel, and covered many subsequent appearances at that venue. I interviewed Nancy Sinatra and some of his other movie co-stars. My path crossed with Elvis' many times, and *Tiger Beat* readers knew, thanks to my "Meow" column, that I was a big Presley fan.

Over the years, my weekly column for *NME* introduced UK readers to the Partridge Family, Freda Payne, Creedence Clearwater Revival, and many more American artists. But by the end of 1971, I was married, doing far less clubbing, and was more involved in the day-to-day editing and production at *Tiger Beat*. I made the difficult decision that my work for *Tiger Beat* should come first, and I stepped away from my *NME* column. While this decision gave me more personal time, I have to admit I missed the extra income. Even more, I missed meeting some of the music business greats, watching the rise of some remarkable talents, and being on the front lines of an amazing time in popular music history.

Chapter 10

My Summer of Love

In April 1966, record producer Lou Adler, then working with the Mamas and the Papas, invited me to one of their Dunhill Records recording sessions. I loved "California Dreamin'" and "Monday, Monday," and I jumped at the chance to meet this super group and get an insider's view of them at work. Their hit songs were the newest California sound, just like the Beach Boys' music had been the soundtrack of surfing.

The atmosphere at United Western Recorders (a complex of studios at 6000 Sunset Boulevard, now known as EastWest Studios) was very casual. Lou, John and Michelle Phillips, Denny Doherty, and Cass Elliot all greeted me warmly as I settled in next to Lou in the engineer's booth. On this day, the foursome was laying down the vocal tracks of "I Saw Her Again," which would go on to be another giant hit for them.

I loved hearing them sing the vocal harmonies over and over again until Lou considered it a "take." At about ten in the evening, we broke for dinner and all sat around Lou's office, Mama Cass on the floor, everyone eating sandwiches and drinking coffee as I interviewed them. Michelle, so tiny and slim, was wearing a darling green mini-dress and knee-high boots, and Cass was wearing what I can only describe as a tent dress, dressed up with love beads and lots of jangly bracelets. Round John-Lennon-type sunglasses completed her look. I have to admit I had never seen such a big girl.

Back in the studio, it was time to do the background vocals. To this day, whenever I hear that song, I remember exactly how they recorded "I Saw Her Again." In the finished recording, you hear them singing "doo, doo, doo," but watching and listening to them record this, I noticed they were also singing "dip, dip, dip" at the same time. For me, it was eye-opening to see how such small details could wind up making a song so much better. Later, I found out that "I Saw Her Again" had been written by John about Michelle's affair with Denny, but probably because I was there as a reporter, any tension among the group got tucked away in my presence. I never would have guessed the real meaning of the song.

About a year later, Lou Adler and John Phillips, along with producer Alan Pariser and my friend Derek Taylor, announced the Monterey International Pop Festival. The three-day event, which later became known as simply the Monterey Pop Festival, is considered the kick-off of what would later be described as the "Summer of Love." I was invited to attend with press credentials, which was thrilling. I figured even if the weekend turned out to be a bust, I loved Monterey and loved being there in that community.

My grandmother lived in Pacific Grove (the little beach town adjacent to Monterey), and my favorite aunt, Aunt Anna, lived in Carmel. Anna was a locally renowned artist, a gourmet cook, and a lover of classical music. From the time I was ten years old, my family spent a week each summer with my grandmother and returned for a week at Thanksgiving. I loved walking the rocks and watching the waves crash at Lovers' Point in Pacific Grove. We'd always have dinner at Anna's house. She was a bit of a recluse and didn't like going out, but my father would bring wine, and Anna always cooked something fabulous. Even before I became a Julia Child fan, I was impressed by Anna's food and saw my first issue of *Gourmet* magazine on her coffee table. I started subscribing to *Gourmet* in 1966.

When I was planning my Monterey festival trip, I arranged to stay with Anna at her tiny, rustic cabin just a block from Ocean Avenue, the main drag of Carmel. I figured it would be easy to commute to and from the festival at the Monterey Fairgrounds via cab. Not such a good assumption.

I flew into Monterey the day before the festival was scheduled to start. I took a cab to Anna's house, and we had a lovely afternoon visit and a delicious Italian dinner. The three-day festival began on Friday, June 16, 1967. The first performances were at 9 p.m., but the Monterey County Fairgrounds opened in the late afternoon, and I headed over, eager to scope out the scene, where dozens of booths were set up with artists selling handmade jewelry, tie-dyed clothing, grass paraphernalia, and food for the hungry crowd. I knew a lot of people who were participating in the festival and kept running into friends and acquaintances.

It was clear to me that this was a true hippie-fest, from the sweet smell of pot in the air to the funky, wild clothing. (The official Monterey International Pop Festival program had set the tone: "Be your own boss. Come as you please, wear what you like. Dress as wild as you choose. But remember that it's sometimes cool in the evenings. Maybe you should bring a blanket and sunglasses.") I hadn't been to a "love-in" before, but at this event, it seemed like we were all family, tied together by music and mutual respect. Even the police officers wore flowers in their uniform caps and on their lapels. No one was busted for openly smoking pot, and there wasn't a single physical altercation the whole weekend. I must have had some kind of contact high, because the entire time, I felt like I was in a dream world—the most perfect place at the perfect time.

I was there for every moment of every performance that weekend. I don't believe everyone on the original program actually appeared—I don't remember seeing the Beach Boys, Dionne Warwick, or the Impressions perform—but that first night, I was thrilled to see the Association, Johnny Rivers, Eric Burdon and the Animals, and Simon and Garfunkel. I had seen them all at least once before, but their shows on this night seemed extra special, somehow. Perhaps it was a sense of being a part of something larger than a solo performance: the awareness that Monterey was one of the first big gatherings of contemporary rock and soul performers. The crowds were excited and enthusiastic, and almost every act got a standing ovation.

After a great night's sleep, I headed back to the fairgrounds for more. Because I was working, I was privileged to be in the press and VIP section—about eight rows of chairs set up right in front of center stage. We were a mixture of press people and rock stars, who'd already performed or were about to, and who wanted to watch their fellow performers from the audience. I've since read that there were many international journalists in attendance. I don't remember meeting any of them, and I always got a chair in one of the first two rows. I also didn't see any of my teen magazine peers—no Gloria Stavers from *16*, no editors from *Flip*, *Tiger Beat*'s newest competitor. I roamed backstage and spent the whole weekend getting great candid shots. I photographed Peter Tork chatting with David Crosby; Brian Jones and his girlfriend in the VIP crowd; Chad Stuart (of Chad and Jeremy) and his wife, Jill; Genie the Tailor with Jefferson Airplane's Paul Kantner; and lots of shots of Paul Simon and Stephen Stills taking their own photos of their friends and fellow rock stars.

I was on my own, but I never felt lonely as I wandered around backstage. Because I'd interviewed many of the festival performers in the past, they were comfortable with me taking candid photos of them. I visited with the stars as a colleague, joining in random conversations before and after the show and between acts. I was amazed that someone like Paul Simon remembered me. I had interviewed him back in my pre-*Tiger Beat* days when he and Art Garfunkel appeared at Melodyland Theater in Anaheim. With a little prompting, he remembered our interview, and we chatted about how far things had come in such a short time, both for Simon and Garfunkel and the pop world in general. The Monterey Pop Festival, we agreed, was proof of that.

As with the performances of the night before, every act on Saturday just seemed more powerful in this festival setting. Janis Joplin was at her wildest during a performance with Big Brother and the Holding Company. I'd seen Janis perform at the Fillmore Auditorium in San Francisco to a crowd of a few hundred. Here, she enthralled an audience of 8,500. Likewise, Country Joe and the Fish, the Butterfield Blues Band, the Byrds, and Jefferson Airplane, who'd all mostly played clubs like the Whisky A Go Go or the Fillmore Auditorium—their performances at Monterey were bigger, and more dramatic. I was blown away by two performers I had never seen in person before: Laura Nyro and Otis Redding. The audience was hushed as they listened to Nyro as she strummed her acoustic guitar and sang intimate, insightful songs with intense lyrics. Redding, who previously had mainly performed for black audiences, was at first uncomfortable with the Monterey audience. He didn't seem to know exactly what to say to us, but he began his set with

"Shake!" As the song got more and more intense, the audience was on its feet shouting and swaying with the music. After Redding got this green light of approval, he thrilled the crowd with his version of Aretha Franklin's "Respect" and a soulful rendition of the Stones' "Satisfaction."

I returned on Sunday afternoon for a solo performance by sitar master Ravi Shankar, who was then all the rage with rock stars, especially the Beatles. I have to admit, I couldn't get into his music. I was bored. After sitting there for about a half hour, I headed backstage, where I shot more great candids and visited with friends like Peter Tork, Genie the Tailor, Spencer Dryden of Jefferson Airplane, and two Raiders, Mike "Smitty" Smith (with his wife) and Phil "Fang" Volk. Micky Dolenz was at the festival all three days, dressed in full Indian buckskins and headdress, but I was never near him long enough to ask why he had chosen that costume for the occasion. He did get a lot of attention—something Micky thrived on.

Rumors flew all weekend that the Beatles were going to make a surprise appearance. I was just as hopeful as every other member of the audience, often looking over my shoulder for any sign of one or more of the Fab Four. But just before he introduced Buffalo Springfield with David Crosby (then of the Byrds), Peter Tork told the audience that the Beatles were *not* appearing.

Brian Jones (who introduced Jimi Hendrix as "the greatest guitarist I've ever seen,") had everyone buzzing about his pink and white flowing robe with the fancy beaded collar. Paul Simon introduced the Mamas and the Papas, and their set, which closed the festival, was magical. Papa John had been instrumental in organizing the festival, and hearing his group's harmonies on "California Dreamin'" being sung right there in Monterey on a summer night was a touching moment for all of us.

The two biggest hits of the festival had to be Jimi Hendrix and the Who. Although I didn't know it at the time, Hendrix and Pete Townshend of the Who argued backstage about who would go on first. According to Townshend, they flipped a coin, and the Who won. Townshend had already become famous for smashing his guitar at the end of every Who performance, and he took his time destroying his guitar at Monterey, too. Not to be outdone, drummer Keith Moon completely demolished his drum kit at the finale. Hendrix followed with a blistering set that ended with "Purple Haze" and a rendition of "Wild Thing" that culminated in Jimi setting his own guitar on fire, then smashing it to bits.

I turned my long weekend into a four-page *Tiger Beat* feature titled "Music, Flowers and Love–The Monterey Pop Festival" with a single column of notes from the weekend and three and a half pages of photos. I was proudest of my photos of Jimi Hendrix and Keith Moon, and once again, I felt incredibly fortunate to be a part of pop culture history.

Photo Gallery

My Disneyland uniform as Head Countergirl at Sunkist "I Presume" in Adventureland.

DC5's Tour Manager, Rick Picone and me.

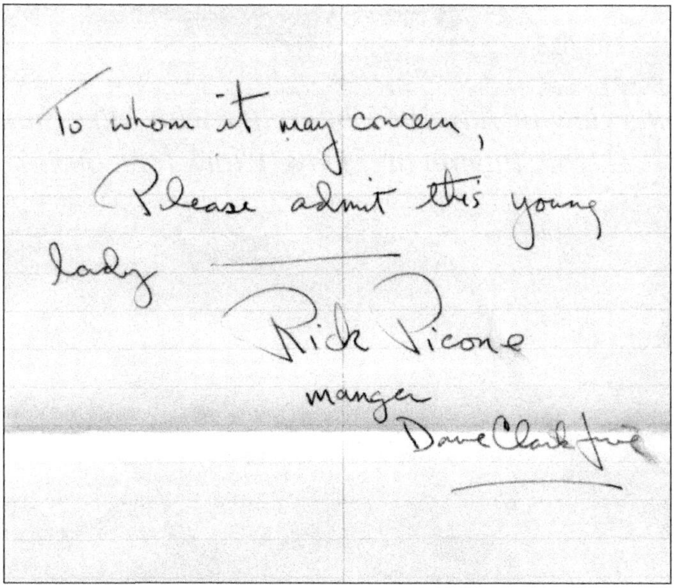

To whom it may concern,
Please admit this young lady ______
Rick Picone
manger
Dave Clark Five

Rick's note that did the trick to allow me backstage at Melodyland.

My interview in July 1965 interview with Mike Smith as Denis Payton and Dave Clark look on.

My photo of Mick Jagger on stage at the Cow Palace, July 1966.

My photo of Brian Jones on stage at the Cow Palace, July 1966.

My mom's "copy" of the Brian Jones jacket, photo taken at Micky's Dolenz' parents home in Los Gatos, CA by Micky's mom.

Jim "Harpo" Valley takes me for a spin during a break in filming "Where The Action Is," 1966.

Sitting at the piano with Mark Lindsay, 1967.

Mark Lindsay and Paul Revere try to ease my anxiety before I deliver my Hollywood Report on "Happening '68."

It worked! Here I get a sincere congratulations from Dick Clark.

Bridget Hanely from "Here Comes the Brides" visits the Tiger Beat offices.

I get a hug from Michael Cole of "The Mod Squad."

Very early in his career, I got a visit from up-and-coming actor Jan Michael Vincent.

Fun times with the Mindbenders during a photo shoot on top of our building at 1800 North Highland Avenue.

Sajid Khan and I say hello at a record company promotion party.

Guaranteed silliness when interviewing Dino, Desi and Billy. This shot taken in the Martin's drive-way.

Dino Martin Jr. turns the tables on me with my tape recorder.

Talking with Billy Hinsche in 1967

The Monkeemobile and me.

Got a portrait of Davy and me during a photo shoot for a Tiger Beat cover.

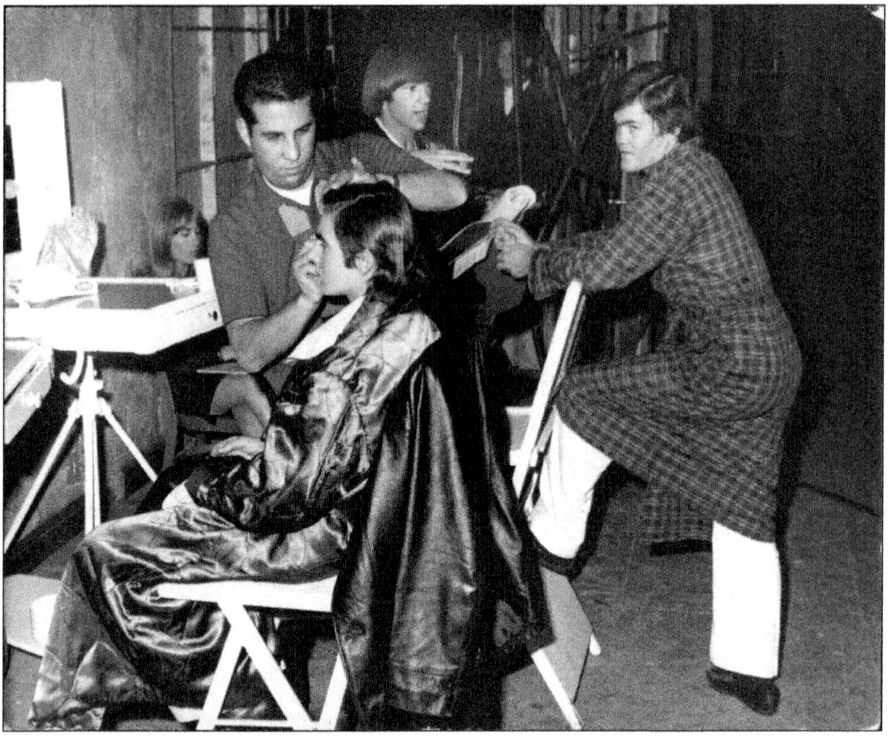

On The Monkees set with Davy, Peter and Micky, and Head Make-up Artist, Maurice Stein.

Peter and I having a "heavy" talk.

One of only a few shots with Michael – this one captured at the open house for his new home in Bel Air. Michael, his manager and me.

On the set of "Head" out at Columbia Ranch with Peter and Micky.

Davy and me (and Andy Payne, boom operator) on the Monkees set. Look closely, you'll see "Photo by Ann Moses" on the back of the photo Davy is checking out.

Davy was great about us recording "At Home with Davy," for a photo essay.

On the Monkees set with visitors
Jim Valley and Chip Douglas.

RALPH L. TUCK
Innkeeper

Holiday Inn® MIDTOWN

PHONE 265-0741

924 MADISON AVENUE • P. O. BOX 1814 • MONTGOMERY, ALABAMA 36103

Dear Mom & Dad,

How the hell are you? Just teasing, Dick said to say that. Dick is the drummer & lead singer in the Standells, who are outtasight as the teenies say. So do I for that matter.

We're here in Montgomery, it's 1:45 and we're watching the Notre Dame, Michigan game on TV. In a little bit I'm going to interview Paul Revere, then I'm taking color shots of Phil Volk... Then... The Standells have asked me to take color shots of them they may want to buy for publicity.

Everything has gone really smoothly. The flight back was rather boring, there was no entertainment and I felt too tired to write any stories.

The shows have been fabulous! And the bus rides are soooooo beautiful. Last tour I was so busy interviewing the Raiders I didn't see any of the countryside. But this time I ride with

HOLIDAY INN EAST
INTERSECTION EASTERN BYPASS AND I-85
MONTGOMERY, ALABAMA

HOLIDAY INN SOUTHWEST
4231 MOBILE HIGHWAY
MONTGOMERY, ALABAMA

My letter to my folks telling them about being on tour

with PR & R and the Standells.

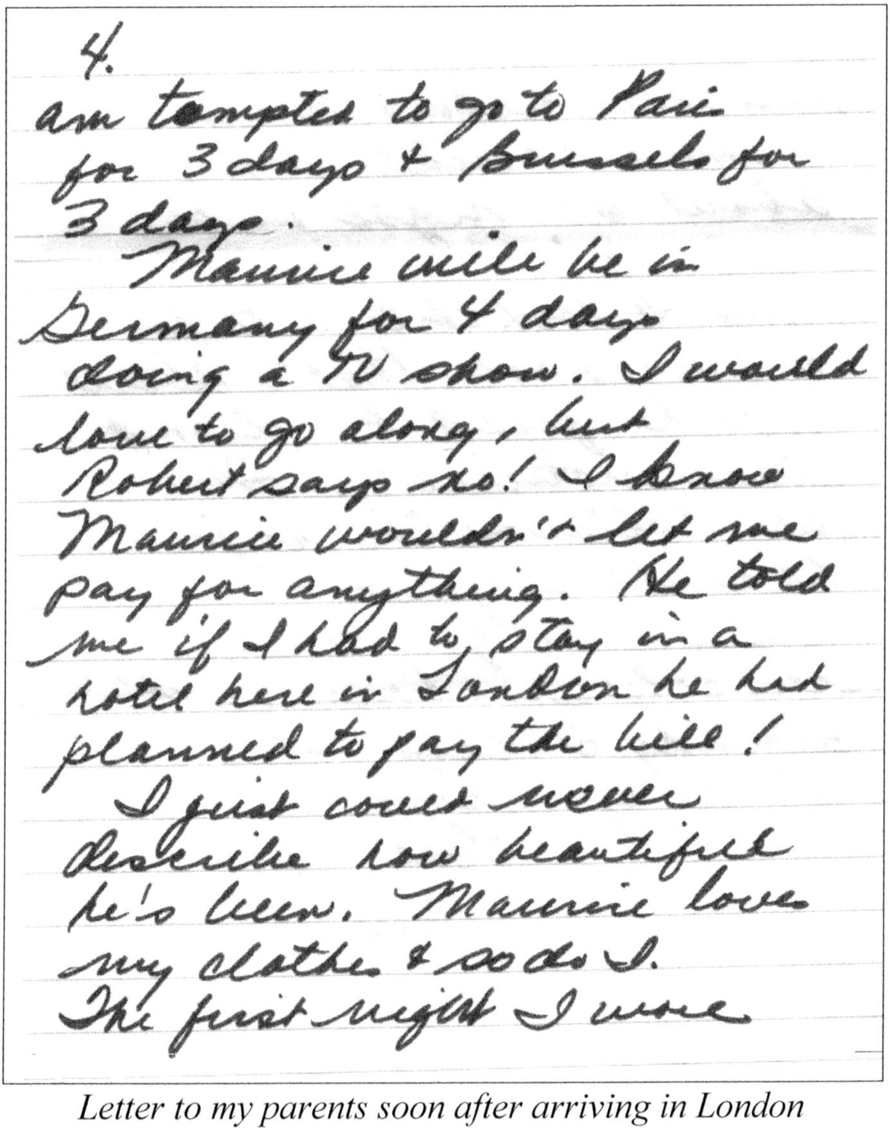

4.

am tempted to go to Paris for 3 days & Brussels for 3 days.

Maurice will be in Germany for 4 days doing a TV show. I would love to go along, but Robert says no! I know Maurice wouldn't let me pay for anything. He told me if I had to stay in a hotel here in London he had planned to pay the bill!

I just could never describe how beautiful he's been. Maurice loves my clothes & so do I. The first night I wore

Letter to my parents soon after arriving in London to stay with Maurice for 3 weeks.

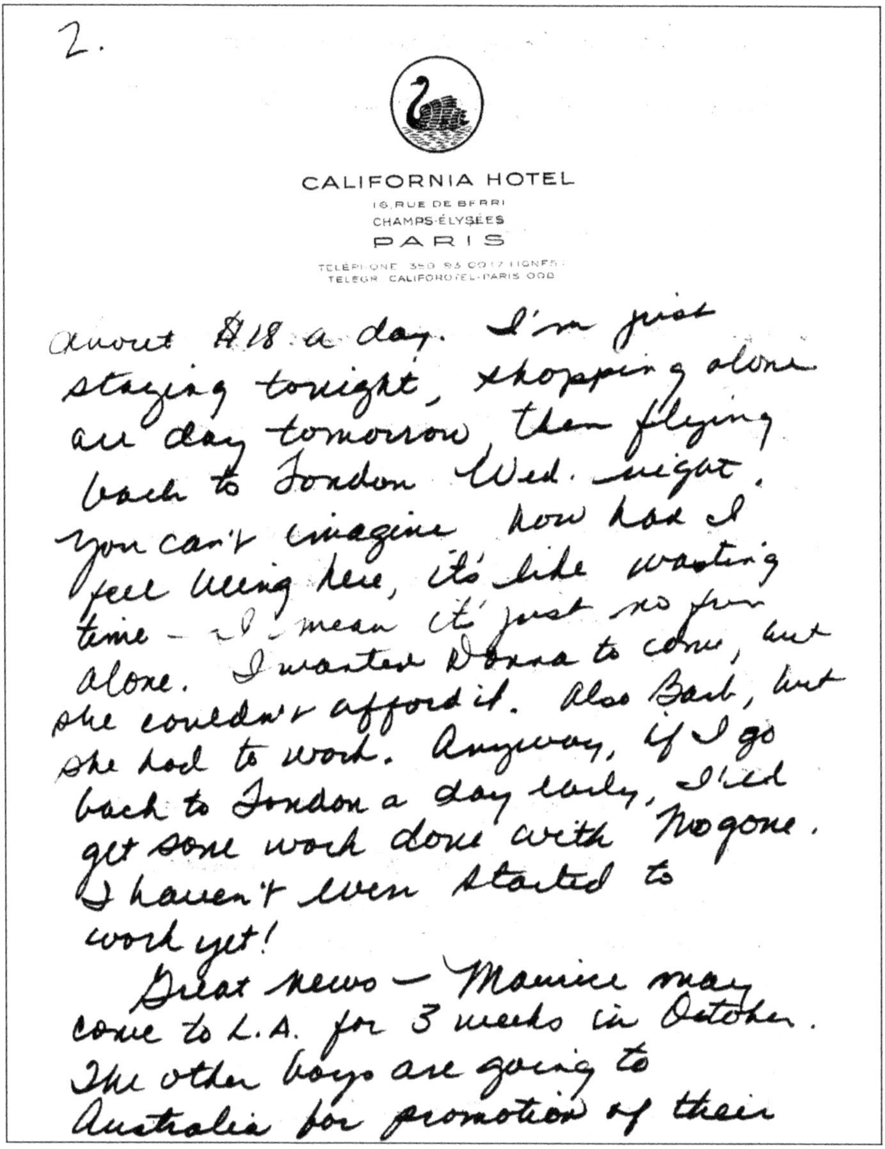

2.

CALIFORNIA HOTEL
16, RUE DE BERRI
CHAMPS-ÉLYSÉES
PARIS
TÉLÉPHONE 359 83 00 (7 LIGNES)
TÉLÉGR. CALIFOROTEL-PARIS 008

about $18 a day. I'm just staying tonight, shopping alone all day tomorrow, then flying back to London Wed. night. You can't imagine how bad I feel being here, it's like wasting time — I mean it's just no fun alone. I wanted Donna to come, but she couldn't afford it. Also Barb, but she had to work. Anyway, if I go back to London a day early, I'll get some work done with Nogone. I haven't even started to work yet!

Great news — Maurice may come to L.A. for 3 weeks in October. The other boys are going to Australia for promotion of their

Letter to Mom and Dad from the California Hotel in Paris.

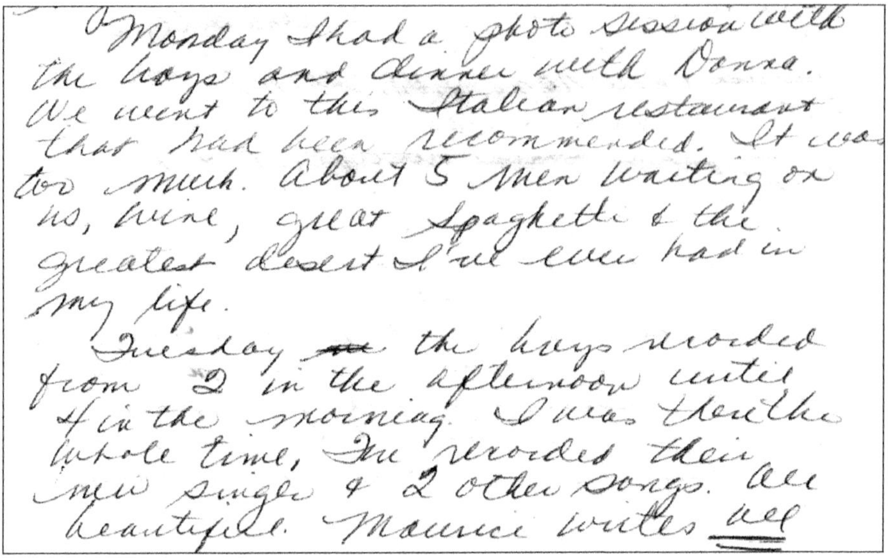
Monday I had a photo session with the boys and dinner with Donna. We went to this Italian restaurant that had been recommended. It was too much. About 5 men waiting on us, wine, great Spaghetti & the greatest desert I've ever had in my life.

Tuesday ~~on~~ the boys recorded from 2 in the afternoon until 4 in the morning. I was there the whole time, They recorded their new single & 2 other songs. All beautiful. Maurice writes all

Another note home toward the end of my trip telling them about the recording session for "Words."

Back to work, having some fun with Susan Cowsill on the tramp after interviewing the family.

The look of love? Maurice looks at me sweetly at the party at Lee Hazelwood's home on February 2, 1968.

My 21st birthday party, my dad shot this Polaroid of Maurice and I "pretending" to celebrate.

Another shot from my dad's Polaroid.

After watching the taping of Elvis' Comeback Special of 1968, I was shocked to find the film editors had superimposed me watching Elvis sing "Can't Help Falling in Love."

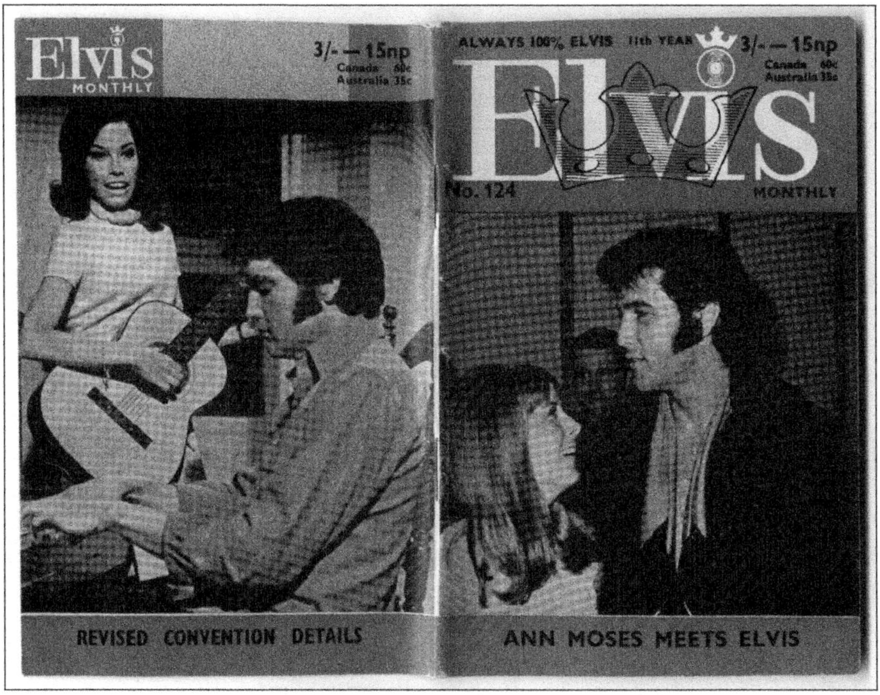

I was thrilled to contribute to Elvis Monthly.

The only way to travel – Bobby always drove the two of us to our luncheon interviews in his Navy Blue Rolls Royce.

Bobby was fabulous about doing portrait shoots for our family of magazines.

This shot was likely taken on the set of Bobby's "Getting Together" series which lasted only one season.

Bobby and I feeding treats to his bloodhounds, Dopey and Goofy.

Another shot of me with Mr. Handsome.

David's 21st birthday party at the Tiger Beat offices.

David and I on set of "The Partridge Family," as he looks over entries to his "Win one of David Cassidy's Puppies" contest.

Me with the "puppies," not long before they were shipped to the winners.

The Osmonds are ready to try my homemade chili for Donny's 14th birthday celebration at my house.

Donny and Marie (before Marie was even performing with her brothers) visit me at the TB offices.

I was in the front row (far left) in my white cocktail dress. Elvis held a rare press conference after his first live appearance at The International.

Photos by Ann Moses, shot on August 1, 1969.

Photos by Ann Moses, shot on August 1, 1969.

Photos by Ann Moses, shot on August 1, 1969.

Photos by Ann Moses, shot on August 1, 1969.

Here's a shot of me during my interview with Denis Sanders, which was one of the segments of "Elvis: That's The Way It Is," a motion picture documentary from 1970.

Poolside with Dave Clark at The Hilton Hotel, Beverly Hills.

Meeting Kurt Russell on the set of
"The One and Only, Genuine, Original Family Band."

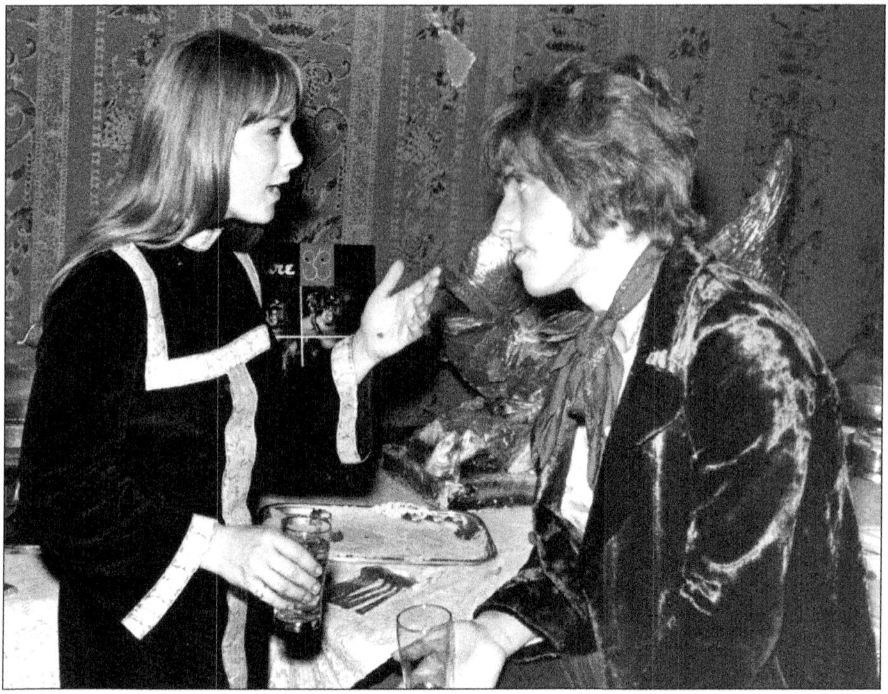

Roger Daltrey and I chat at the debut party of one of the Who's albums.

Jack Wild, while he played the Artful Dodger in the movie version of "Oliver," he was a nice kid, but could never match up to Davy Jones, try as his managers might.

Here's a fave shot of Peter Noone saying hello as he gets off the plane in Hollywood.

Chapter 11

How to Fall in Love Without Really Trying

When I headed out to interview the Bee Gees one warm July afternoon in 1967, it was just another *Tiger Beat* assignment, covering the latest cute guy band. Who knew my life was about to change? Not me. As with every interview I did, I was excited to be meeting someone new. What would they be like? Stuck up? Humble? Full of themselves? Funny?

At the Bee Gees' hotel room, manager Robert Stigwood (known as Stiggy to most of his clients) introduced me to Barry, Robin, and Robin's fraternal twin, Maurice (pronounced "Morris" in England), as well as the other two members of the band at that time, Vince Melouney and Colin Petersen. Stiggy suggested we do our interview out on the balcony in the beautiful warm California sunshine.

While most performers were comfortable and outgoing on stage, as young men new to the "star" game, they were sometimes shy and unsure of themselves offstage. The Bee Gees weren't like this. They were playful, cracked jokes, and turned our two-hour interview into a lighthearted afternoon.

The group had scored hits in Australia and England, but where America was concerned, the Bee Gees were still in the "honeymoon" stage. This would be my first article on the group for *Tiger Beat*, so I did a lot of the usual, basic-profile stuff with each of them individually, as well as a group. Barry and Maurice were usually the first to answer the questions I threw out.

I never set out to "hook up" with any of the guys I interviewed; that just wasn't my style. To be honest, most of them had girlfriends—models, actresses, singers—much prettier and more hip than I. And if they didn't have girlfriends, they had groupies with big boobs just a phone call away. But when I interviewed the Bee Gees, something happened I'd never experienced before. Not only did Maurice and I have nearly constant eye contact, but the way he smiled at me sent a charge through me that was new and unexpected. His flirting caught me totally off guard. I don't think I even recognized it as flirting. All I knew was, I was really attracted to this guy.

After we finished the interview, Maurice asked me to walk out with the group, who were headed to a television taping. As we neared the doors of the hotel lobby, Maurice turned to face me, stepped close, and held my Indian bead necklace in his hand, close to my thumping heart. I breathed in his wonderful scent. He smelled heavenly, like jasmine—exotic and sexy.

"That necklace is so cool. Where did you get it?" he said.

I managed to stammer out the words, "I made it myself on a loom. Would you like me to make one for you?"

“Yes! Would you?” He asked for some paper from my reporter’s notebook, and scribbled down his London address, then squeezed my shoulder and said, “I can’t wait to see what colors you pick out for me.” And he was gone, catching up with the rest of the guys as they climbed into their limo.

As I drove back to the office, I couldn’t shake the warm tingles flowing through me. Instead of heading back to the office—I was too “high” from my exchange with Maurice—I stopped at a craft store and picked out beads for the necklace I would begin as soon as I got home that evening.

During the next few days, I managed to stay focused at work. I met my deadlines and hung out on the *Monkees* set. Once home, I didn’t have much idle time. I finished Maurice’s necklace in colors of red, brown, gold, and white—very much like the necklace I’d worn to our interview. I wrapped it as a present, put in a brief note saying I hoped he liked it, and sent it via air mail, which I knew would take about two weeks.

I had written plenty of gushy articles about how faves love-love-loved and cherished handmade gifts from fans, but I knew that this wasn’t, for the most part, always true. More often than not, a secretary unwrapped gifts and opened fan mail, and since no grownup pop star wanted or needed 137 teddy bears or whatever, these gifts were usually forwarded somewhere other than to the star himself. I figured the most I’d get in response to my necklace gift would be a nice note from a secretary on Robert Stigwood stationery.

Boy, was I was wrong.

One August morning, I was awakened by the telephone ringing at 5 a.m.

"Annie! It's Maurice! I love my necklace! You're amazing!"

My first transatlantic phone call. It's Maurice Gibb, and he's calling me! I was awake in a shot.

"I'm so glad," I said calmly, but my heart was pounding so loud, I was sure he could hear it over 5,000 miles away. I was breathing so hard, I had to cover the mouthpiece with my hand as he spoke.

Maurice told me he was calling from the recording studio. "What time is it there?" I asked.

"About one in the afternoon. We're just having a tea break." He asked me what I was doing that day, and I told him I was going to a Jefferson Airplane recording session. We talked about their music for a while, until Maurice was called back into the studio.

Needless to say, I couldn't get back to sleep. Butterflies were dancing the Watusi in my stomach. I turned the lights on, sat on the bed, and replayed our phone call over and over in my brain.

About a week later, I got another 5 a.m. wake-up call. A transatlantic call of fifteen or twenty minutes would have cost Maurice about £135, the equivalent of over $300 in 1967. This time we chatted casually, like new friends eager to get to know one another. A few days later, he called again. Maurice never ended a call by saying he'd talk to me again, but he kept calling. Those first few calls, we talked about his family, and he told me how he'd tried to buy a farm in the countryside. The deal hadn't gone through, so he was still living with his parents, his younger brother, Andy, and his grandmother. He'd describe the new suit he'd just bought—Maurice was a real clothes horse—or how he'd had the windows on his Mini Cooper tinted.

Right around this time, I was in the process of moving from my studio apartment into a rented house just below the famous Hollywood sign, the former home of our *Tiger Beat* art director, Norbert Jobst. It was such a cool house, probably built around 1950, with a huge living room, a beautiful white stone fireplace, a dining room with wood floors, and a really big kitchen. A dramatic staircase led to the two upstairs bedrooms. Norbert sold me some of his furniture, including a fantastic lime green velvet tufted sofa. I bought some glass coffee tables and thrift store lamps, and my mom found a carved walnut queen headboard, a solid walnut dresser, and a gorgeous green and gold filigree mirror—all for $300. I sewed my own bedspread, made of long white fake fur. It was 1967, after all.

My first night in my new home, I had such a peaceful night's sleep, cozy under my furry bedspread. Maurice's call awoke me at 5 a.m. After our usual chitchat of fifteen or twenty minutes, he took me by surprise. "I would love it if you'd come to England for a visit—do you think you'd be able to take a vacation from work?"

I didn't know what to say. I knew Chuck would love the chance for me to take a working vacation in London, covering all the UK faves who were so hot at the time. Maurice was asking me to come for three weeks. I wanted to scream "Yes!" right on the spot, but instead I told him, "Let me check with my boss, and I'll let you know."

This time, he gave me his number and said, "Call me as soon as you can. I want to see you!" No boy or man had ever treated me so special.

It took me about two days to work out the details with Ralph and Chuck. There were, of course, upcoming publication deadlines that had to be met, but once we got that squared away, I was on the phone with a travel agent later that same day. In those days, you could get a "triangle" or "rectangle" fare, meaning instead of just flying round trip to London, you could also fly to three other European cities for the same price. I signed up for a rectangle, because I wanted to visit a friend from high school who was working in Brussels, and I was hoping Maurice and I might go somewhere else outside of London. I daydreamed about the two of us strolling along the Seine in Paris, walking hand in hand and taking silly photographs in front of the Eiffel Tower.

There'd been no discussion of where I would stay or what we would do over the three weeks I'd be there; I just assumed Maurice would be in charge, that he was a man who knew his way around London and beyond. My head was in the clouds, and I was more interested in my mom making me some new clothes for the trip than I was in what would transpire once I arrived. We scoured the newest Vogue pattern books, and she made me a navy pinstriped pantsuit, a beautiful light pink wool mini-dress, and a white wool coat—all the latest Paris designs. They were gorgeous. I also packed my favorite pantsuit, made by my friend Genie the Tailor, a purple-striped number with a frilly collared shirt that filled the "V" of the jacket. Mom had already made a black velvet caftan with gold embroidered trim on the collar and sleeves. Caftans were the height of India-inspired fashion, as were Nehru jackets.

My flight touched down at Heathrow Airport three hours late. I felt terrible about Maurice waiting there all that time. Before any of the passengers left their seats, a representative from the airline came on board and called out "Miss Ann Moses?" I raised my hand timidly. He explained he would "take care of everything," then escorted me off the plane, through the coach section, and past the first class passengers.

As I wrote in a letter to my parents: "Really the red carpet treatment. He led me through immigration; being the first one off the plane made it go very fast, then the man got my bags and escorted me through customs. On the other side of the automatic doors leading out of customs stood Maurice. He looked drop-dead gorgeous, and even from a distance I could see the necklace I had made him around his neck. As soon as I walked up to him, he gave me a huge hug and a kiss on the cheek. My idea of a mind-blowing reception!"

At the airport curb, the airline guy placed my bags in the trunk of a black Rolls Royce sedan with a driver behind the wheel. Maurice had not been to bed; he'd been at the Speakeasy Club with John and Cynthia Lennon until 5 a.m. The car was John's; he had loaned it to Maurice to pick me up at the airport.

"I didn't think your luggage would fit in my Mini Cooper," Maurice deadpanned.

My mind was reeling. *I, Ann Moses, am in London, England. I've just had my first transatlantic flight, and now I'm riding in a Rolls Royce owned by one of the Beatles, and I'm visiting the most beautiful man I've ever been close to—a real rock star.* I felt like I was in the middle of the best dream of my life. All the *Tiger Beat* exclamation points in the world couldn't do justice to how I felt at that moment.

Once we were in the back seat of the limo, Maurice grabbed my hand and didn't let go for our entire ride. Here we were, two people who had met once and talked on the phone a few times, but I felt like he was my longtime boyfriend, not a stranger. Everything was so comfortable between us, if you didn't count the electric current flashing through every nerve ending in my body. He sat close to me, and there was that smell of jasmine again, just like the day we met.

The driver didn't speak as we headed for a tour of downtown London. We were stopped by a London Bobbie as we passed Buckingham Palace, and we had a front row seat for the

Changing of the Guard. Maurice beamed as I watched this centuries-old tradition in amazement.

"You're quite the tour guide," I teased him.

"And you thought it was the airline that delayed your plane!" he replied.

Even as we passed the London Bridge and Trafalgar Square and numerous British monuments, I kept looking down at our hands entwined and felt such a closeness with him. How could this be, when we'd only known each other for such a short time? My brain couldn't make sense of what my heart was feeling. I wasn't just in a different time zone, I was on a different planet!

Finally, we made our way out to the suburbs of London, where Maurice lived. His folks were warm and welcoming, and after a brief visit with them, Maurice and I headed out to do some clothes shopping. On our way to Dandy Fashions in Chelsea, Maurice stopped at the bank and deposited a royalty check for £1000, which was about $2500 US dollars. Such a rock star thing to do. He bought lots of great gear, and, after shopping, we drove to a small town about a hundred miles away, where the Bee Gees were performing that night at a small community center with enough room for about 150 people to stand —an appearance booked before the Bee Gees had scored two worldwide hits. On that leisurely drive to the venue, we talked and laughed, and Maurice often tenderly touched my knee. Peeking out the window, I got wonderful glimpses of English countryside villages.

We still hadn't talked about where I would be staying. "I've made arrangements at home for you to stay with us," Maurice finally said. "But if you'd rather stay at a hotel, I'll pay all your expenses. I just want you to be comfortable."

I was touched that he wanted me to stay with his family rather than at a hotel, miles away from him. Besides, I wanted to spend every minute I could with him!

The show that night was fantastic. By then, the Bee Gees were playing to crowds of 5,000 and more, so a show in this intimate venue was really special. As I stood next to the stage, it occurred to me that I was living the fantasy I wrote about for all the young girls who read *Tiger Beat*. "All these fans are going crazy for the Bee Gees," I couldn't help but think, "but I'm going home with Maurice."

On the way home from the show, we stopped and ordered my very first real fish and chips, served in a newspaper cone. They were marvelous. We got back to London about 2:30 a.m. and headed straight for the Speakeasy Club for a couple of drinks. The legal drinking age in California was twenty-one, and I was just twenty, so I wasn't much of a drinker. I'd had the occasional glass of wine or cocktail at a press party. Maurice liked rum and Coke, so that's what we drank.

Neither of us had been to bed for forty-eight hours, so the alcohol just made me sleepy. We got home about 5 a.m. Someone had set up a cot for Maurice in a downstairs bedroom, and I was given Maurice's bedroom, with a single bed and his clothes hanging all over the place. In British row houses, there were no closets, just freestanding wardrobes. And no single wardrobe could hold Maurice's incredible collection of casual clothes and stage costumes.

Maurice walked me up the stairs to his room and kissed me tenderly on the lips, again and again. "Good night. I'm so glad you are here!" he said, then closed the door before heading down to his cot. It was all so innocent and perfect, like some kind of really great *Tiger Beat* fantasy.

We slept until three the next afternoon. His mum cooked us an authentic English breakfast—eggs over easy, tomatoes, English bacon, mushrooms, and toast—served with lots of hot tea, which I drank just as Maurice did, with milk and sugar.

That afternoon, we visited a nearby record store, goofing off like teenagers. Then we were off to another Bee Gees performance in another small town 130 miles away. Driving through the picturesque English countryside was just as exciting as it had been the day before. This time, though, Maurice would occasionally pull off the roadside so we could make out.

"I can't resist you," he said, leaving me speechless and stunned by his attention. What a good kisser he was! I'd had a steady boyfriend in high school and had dated a few others, and had lost my virginity the year before to what turned out to be a one-night stand. But I was still very naive about sex. Maurice's kissing expertise was very much appreciated.

After the show, we headed back to London and the Speakeasy Club, where we talked for hours. No topic was off limits. Maurice told me he thought Paul McCartney's girlfriend, Jane Asher, was awfully stuck-up. He called her a "cunt." I had never heard this word before, and asked shyly what it meant. He showed me by pointing. "It's like calling a guy a prick," he explained.

We got home at 5 a.m. He came up to "my" room and sat on the bed, and we talked and made out until 8:30 a.m. We woke at five the next evening, and I needed to wash my hair. There was no shower, so I figured out how to lather up my long hair and dunk my head into the bath water until the soap was out.

That night, we went to the Saville Theatre to see John Mayall and the Bluesbreakers. Maurice held my hand tenderly as he led me to the late Brian Epstein's private box for the evening's performance, and I wanted to enjoy the music—I was a blues fan by this time—but everything was a blur. My mind was reeling, thinking about where I was and with whom. I was also distracted by Maurice's extremely tight trousers. I couldn't keep my eyes off his rather prominent "package."

It was nearly midnight when we got home. "Why don't you go up and put on your pajamas," he suggested, "and then come back downstairs."

The moment was upon me. In all the hubbub of preparing for my trip, I'd never given a thought to starting birth control pills again. I know it sounds dumb, but I somehow hadn't envisioned us being that intimate. Now, the pressure was on.

I went upstairs and changed into my babydoll pajamas, then I tiptoed down the stairs as quietly as I could. The only light in the room was the streetlight through the sheer curtains. Maurice was under the covers, and he scooted over a little on the cot and lifted the sheets for me. I lay down beside him. He held me tightly in his arms, and we kissed more passionately than before. He finally said, "Are you sure you want to do this?"

I nodded.

"Have you ever done this before?" he said.

I lied again. "No."

I thought it was important to a man that he be the first. Soon, we were kissing, and he pulled off the bottoms of my babydolls and his own low-rise briefs. He lay on top of me, and I could feel his erection pressing into my belly. "I'll pull out so you won't get pregnant," he whispered to me. Man, were we young. And naïve!

Afterward, we lay together for a few minutes, not speaking, then he handed me my pajama bottoms. I took that as my cue that we were finished. I slipped them on, snuck back up the stairs, and closed my door as quietly as I could.

I had thought our mutual attraction would equal passionate lovemaking, even though I had no idea what passionate lovemaking actually involved. Neither did Maurice, as it turned out. So, besides being sore, I was disappointed. Where were the fireworks?

We really were just two inexperienced kids. Neither of us knew about foreplay, fondling, oral sex. Fortunately, Maurice didn't know enough to be disappointed in me, and our closeness only intensified.

The next morning, Maurice was due at a London radio station where the Bee Gees were doing a live interview, so I went shopping on Carnaby Street with my friend Mike Hewitson, a roadie for the Dave Clark Five. I bought presents for my Hollywood friends, like Nehru jackets for $9, and we had lunch at a vegetarian restaurant.

That night, Maurice and I stayed home, had a simple dinner, and watched TV and home movies with his family. The movies were of family vacations, as well as early Bee Gees performances when the group was just the three Gibb brothers. There were also movies of the boys' older sister, Lesley, who performed in nightclubs as an exotic dancer in a sparkly, skimpy costume, draped in live snakes.

"His family is nice, except he has his niece here who's three and a little nuisance to have around," I wrote to my folks back home. "Also a 'cheeky' nine-year-old brother (Andy Gibb!). His other brothers have flats of their own."

Maurice and I stayed up until everyone had gone to bed, and once the house was quiet, climbed into his cot for another go at sex. This time as we were talking he said, "I've heard some of the guys say that sometimes a girl will put her mouth on a guy's thing. Isn't that weird?"

I had never heard of a blow job before. Maurice didn't appear to be suggesting I attempt this unusual act; in fact, he sounded grossed out by it. Maybe he was too chicken to say, "You want to try it?" Thank God he didn't. I was so not there yet.

The next night, we stayed in our respective beds. Sometime in the middle of the night, I heard screaming from the next room. I ran to open my door.

"You go back to bed, dear," Mrs. Gibb said. "It's Grandma. She's gotten stuck on her chamber pot. I'll take care of her."

I went back to bed. *Chamber pot?* I thought. *Really?*

The next morning we'd planned to drive out to Kent, in the countryside, to watch the Beatles filming *Magical Mystery Tour*. I couldn't believe I would be meeting the Beatles! But it rained all day, and the shoot was cancelled. Damn it. (I've since read that, by this time, principal filming was finished, but maybe Maurice thought it was still going on.)

Instead, we drove into London and hung around on Carnaby Street, the epicenter of Swingin' London, where I spent the afternoon discovering more of the wonders of the hippest place on earth. There were cool shops everywhere: Mod Male, owned by hip menswear designer John Stephen, as well as Mates Boutique, Lady Jane, Lord John, and Gear Boutique—all of which became instant faves. Pop Boutique, which was the first to sell Union Jack shirts, was a revelation. We stopped in at 21

Shop, owned by famous mod designer Mary Quant, who described her clothing designs as "simple, zany, not for squares." Biba made a statement with loud music, dimly lit interiors, stylish staff, and the clothing of famed clothier Barbara Hulanicki. I was surprised when Maurice explained how these shops used to be stuffy department stores, because the Carnaby Street of 1967 was now its own world of pop art murals, with wild colors of purple, yellow, and red all over the facades, the marquees, and the clothing.

No one seemed to take notice of Maurice, the pop star, because the unique vibe on Carnaby Street was that this was the place for rock stars and commoners alike to shop, hang out, and people-watch. On later shopping trips, I made several gift purchases, and I even loved the paper shopping bags (or "carry bags," as the British called them) covered with Union Jacks, wild paisley prints, and other pop art.

We ended most nights with a nightcap at the Speakeasy, where many of the rock stars hung out, although we seldom saw anyone famous there. We always had our most serious talks there, somehow. That night, Maurice confided that he didn't like how Paul McCartney "slept around" when he had a girlfriend. "If I were engaged or married," he said, "I would never sleep around." He talked about wanting to get married someday and have children, and I told him I felt the same. I couldn't believe he was the one bringing up this subject.

The next day, the Bee Gees were appearing on *Top of the Pops* and were meeting at Stiggy's flat before the show. Stiggy's place was decorated in wild animal skins and African décor, but I wasn't there long enough to look around. Maurice handed me the keys to his car and said, "I'll be about two hours. Why don't you go for a drive?"

Me? Driving with a left-handed stick shift...on the wrong side of the road?

I gathered my courage, gave him a swift kiss good-bye, and got out of his hair. I sat in the car for a long time, trying to get comfortable with the gearshift and with sitting on the "wrong" side of the car. Finally, I just thought, "What the hell," and slowly pulled out into traffic. I did pretty well until I got to Piccadilly Circus, one of the busiest roundabouts in London. I was totally turned around, and pretty soon there were cars coming straight at me, honking. I bolted to attention when I heard the high-pitched squeal of a bobbie's whistle. I was going the *wrong* way! I slammed on the brakes as the other cars careened around me, some coming to noisy, screeching stops.

I slammed down the accelerator as the bobbies descended on me, yelling and chasing me on foot. I managed to lose them, and once I had, I pulled to the side of the road and began to sob.

What if I had crashed Maurice's car? What if I'd been hurt? What if I'd been arrested or hurt someone else?

After a good cry, I checked my map, calculated my way back to Stiggy's flat, and parked outside. I sat there with my eyes closed until Maurice came out an hour later.

"Have you been waiting long?" he asked.

"Not really," I said. Then I told Maurice my harrowing traffic story, which caused him to burst out laughing. And I began to cry again.

He could see at this point how truly frightened I was, both about what had happened and about the humiliation of having to confess it. I felt like a dope.

"Don't cry, baby. I'm just glad you're okay," he said. "Wasn't it a Brit who said 'All's well that ends well'?" He held me tightly in his arms, and I felt a lot better. But I didn't drive again in London for a long time after that.

The next day, the guys had a concert at Pacific Hall at Wolverhampton—no girlfriends allowed. I decided after days of guilty pleasure (and not doing a lick of work) to get some *Tiger Beat* writing done. I scheduled lunch in London with Basil Foster, who'd given Davy Jones his big break in show business, and took my first ride on the "tube," the underground rail system that can take you anywhere in London. We were joined by Unity Hall, the editor of *Fabulous* magazine. She was so much a part of swingin' London, and I wanted to be just like her.

Maurice and his brothers were busy preparing for performances in Germany, so I spent the next couple days exploring London. I visited the Victoria and Albert Museum, where I spent hours looking at royal gowns, silver, jewelry, and other wonderful old stuff, and the Tower of London, where I saw the Crown Jewels. I met *New Musical Express* editor Andy Gray at a traditional English pub and pitched him on the idea of giving me a full-time job. I walked for miles, trying to find the famous Portobello Road Market in the west end of London, and somehow I ended up in the red light district of Soho, where men muttered "Cute bird!" and "You wanna go for a pint?" as I passed them.

This is where I bumped into my good friend from Hollywood, Donna Mondorea. We'd met when she was dating Curt Boettcher, the producer of the Association, whom I'd interviewed for *Tiger Beat*. I hadn't seen her for months, and here we were, bumping into one another in London's red light district.

That night, Maurice and I attended the first UK appearance of Traffic. The group—Steve Winwood, Jim Capaldi, Chris Wood, and Dave Mason—had recently released their first single, and we were excited to hear them perform live.

Maurice and I were alone in a private booth, having a lovely chat. Just seconds before the show began, the curtains to our box flew open and in walked Lulu, accompanied by her manager. Lulu was hugely popular in Britain, having gained fame in the film *To Sir, with Love* with Sidney Poitier. She said a quick hello and sat down behind us. After the show ended, Lulu asked Maurice if we'd like to join them for dinner.

Maurice told me he'd met Lulu once before at the Speakeasy Club, but they'd never dated. We joined Lulu at a fancy restaurant, where she was as bubbly in person as she was onstage. All blazing red hair and cockney accent, she leaned over and whispered into Maurice's ear—a lot. I thought it was very uncool, but Maurice continued to be attentive to me, smiling and stroking my knee under the table. It was 1967, and I'd never encountered a "mean girl" before, or one who was so aggressive.

When Maurice excused himself to go to the men's room, Lulu dropped her friendly façade. She leaned close to me, looked me straight in the eye, and said, in a steely tone, "When you're gone, *I'll* be the one dating Maurice."

I was too stunned to respond. What I was thinking was, *You fucking cunt!* But Maurice was back at the table before I had a chance to really answer Lulu's bitchy challenge. Luckily, our dinner was drawing to a close.

As we walked out of the restaurant, my confusion must have shown on my face, because Maurice looked concerned and asked, "Are you all right?"

"I'm just tired," I lied.

Outside, I was grateful for the chill in the air as I wrapped my new wool coat around my shoulders. I was thankful, too, for Maurice's arm wrapped tightly around me as we walked to his car.

I never told him about Lulu's rude threat, which had stirred up every insecurity I had about how Maurice could possibly be interested in me. Looking back, I always wonder what would have happened—to him, to me, to us—if I'd told my new boyfriend about what that bitch had said to me.

Her words would come back to slap me in the face, soon enough.

Chapter 12

An American Girl in Paris

Maurice left the next morning for Germany to tape an appearance on *Der Goldene Schub*, a big-deal German TV show. Stiggy made it clear that this was a "boys only" trip, so I saw Maurice off at the airport, then spent the day running around with Donna. We found a really great Italian restaurant for dinner, where I ate my very first Croquembouche. I'd never seen anything like it before. When the waiter brought the towering dessert to the table, I just stared.

"Do we eat the whole thing?" I asked.

He was very gracious as he explained that we should help ourselves to as many of the cream puffs as we thought we wanted. They were delicious.

After dinner, Donna dropped me at the airport. Because Maurice would be gone for the next few days, I'd arranged flights to see my friend Barbara in Brussels, then on to Paris and Amsterdam for a little solo exploring as part of my "rectangle" plane ticket.

In Brussels, I browsed the Grand Plaza and the shops, which after London I found pretty boring. Brussels was beautiful, but being alone and not speaking the language was a drag. Barbara and I met for dinner that night, and we got caught up on each other's lives. She admitted she was jealous of my life and, frankly, I was jealous of hers: She'd ventured out and was living in Europe, discovering new places. As memorable (and surprising!) as that conversation was, the thing I remember most about our dinner was the pork roast dish I ordered. These European meals, in the summer of 1967, were really my introduction to gourmet cuisine, a hobby I've cultivated and enjoyed ever since.

I begged Barbara to join me in Paris, but she had to work and couldn't afford a plane ticket. I was on my own once again.

The English-speaking concierge at Charles de Gaulle airport helped me find a room: on the Champs-Elysees, and just $18 for the night. The room was gorgeous, with an overstuffed canopy bed and doors that led out to a balcony with a view of the Arc de Triomphe.

I was in the most romantic city in the world, and I was alone. Rather than going exploring, I—insecure about being in a foreign country where I didn't know the language—sat down and wrote a letter to my parents, told them it was no fun being alone and that I might go back to London to get some work done.

"Great news," I wrote. "Maurice may come to LA for three weeks in November. You might have guessed we're very much in love. Maurice told me to write and tell you he loves me, so I am. You'll love him, I just know it."

Even as I wrote these words, I again asked myself: "Why me? How could this amazing man pay me so much attention, be so charming and loving toward me with his caresses and kisses? Is it possible he's romancing me to get coverage in *Tiger Beat*?"

It seemed ludicrous to me that *Tiger Beat,* out of dozens of magazines, could be so important, but I knew enough to know the idea had merit. I was consumed with a feeling of being "less" than the beautiful girls who surrounded rock stars. My belly wasn't flat, so I wore my hip huggers higher than skinny girls like Cher, who had helped popularize them, always did. I obsessed about the gargantuan zit that had appeared below my lower lip about two days before my flight, and I did everything possible to cover it with concealer for the first few days. These might have been the same anguishes of most girls my age, but I couldn't rationalize that Maurice seemed to be falling for me.

Despite my insecure musings, I had a dreamy night's sleep in my elegant bed, with the French doors open to let in the cool breeze. In the morning, I indulged in a comforting bath in the enormous, antique claw-foot tub, then ordered corn flakes and orange juice from room service. It breaks my heart today when I think that I didn't head out into Paris, walking until I discovered the scent of freshly baked croissants, but once again, I was intimidated by the language. After breakfast, I dressed in my pink wool mini-dress and the new navy shoes I had bought in London. I felt very chic.

Barbara had told me the best place in Paris for shopping was the Boulevards de Saint Germain, so I made my way to the subway and bought a ticket. After the train pulled out, a man in uniform made his way through the car taking tickets. He snatched mine from my hand and began screaming at me in French. When we pulled in to the next station, he grabbed my arm and pushed me off the train. He was still yelling as I stood on the platform, dumbfounded, as the train pulled out of the station. A French woman overheard the scene and came up to me and said, "Let me see your ticket."

I showed her the stub, and she explained, "The Metro has first class and second class cars. Your ticket is for second class, and you boarded a first class car."

Well. Excuse me!

When I finally got to the Boulevards de Saint Germain, I found the shops and sidewalk cafés just beautiful. I really had my mind set on buying a fabulous pair of black leather boots, and when I found a shoe shop, I communicated with the clerk by using sign language. Those boots, made of soft, supple leather, had a fashionable square toe and low, two-inch heels. They cost me only $45, and I wore those boots for years.

I finally gathered up all my courage and sat down in a street café. I ordered steak and French fries. I groan, thinking about it now: I'm in a gourmet's paradise, and I order the most American dish I can find. It was cooked to perfection, though, and as I sat contemplating my next excursion, I decided I didn't want to fly to Amsterdam and spend another day not being able to converse with people.

I took the Metro back to my hotel, checked out, and took a cab to the airport, where I caught the next flight back to London. I called the Gibbs and let them know I would be home before nine. "That will be lovely, dear," Mrs. Gibb said. They were such gracious hosts.

My famous boyfriend was still in Germany, so I did what any young American girl would have done in my position: I called a famous rock band and asked to spend the day with them on the set of the movie they were shooting.

I'd become good friends with Herman's Hermits even before I began working at *Tiger Beat*. I'd met them while I was writing for *Rhythm 'n' News*, and had briefly dated bass player Karl Green during one of their visits to California. Our dates never led to a real romance, but we'd remained friends. On this trip, all the Hermits were so sweet and seemed really happy to see me. Karl introduced me to his new bride, who was also there to watch the band shoot *Mrs. Brown, You've Got a Lovely Daughter*.

Later, we all went to the historic Coach Inn where the band was staying and had a delicious lunch of fresh fish. When I was a kid, my mom would allow me to go to Pink's Drive-In and buy myself a hamburger whenever she prepared fish for dinner. She knew I hated fish and never forced me to eat it. On this day, the chef at this fine establishment changed my opinion of fish forever. Another funny memory from that trip is how the door frames at the Inn were so low, the boys had to bend over to get through without bumping their heads.

I met Maurice back at the Gibbs' house that afternoon. He was exhausted from the Germany trip, but he came up to "my" room. "I want to get us a hotel room for the weekend," he whispered. "I'll tell my parents we're going horse riding in the country and will be staying out there. I want to be alone with you!"

Talk about romantic! I was speechless, but managed to say, "That sounds wonderful."

The next afternoon, we took off, eventually stopping off at an elegant establishment called the Thistle Piccadilly Hotel on Coventry Street. Trafalgar Square was just down the road. A valet in a fancy waistcoat and hat opened my door, and I tried to exit discreetly from the Mini Cooper—thank goodness I was wearing one of my pantsuits. Maurice grabbed my hand as we approached the front desk clerk. "Do you have a reservation, sir?" asked the clerk.

"No," Maurice said. "I'd like a room for Mr. and Mrs. Robert Andrews." (I don't know where he got that name from—maybe Robert from Robert Stigwood? And Andrews from little brother Andy?) In those days, a hotel in London's posh West End would never have rented a room to an unmarried couple. Even though Maurice was holding my hand, I trembled as I thought back to the night I was almost thrown out of a

Baltimore hotel when Harpo showed me to my room. Maurice was a contradiction: a naïve teenager just learning about sex and love, yet commanding in his confidence as he booked us a room. He didn't have a credit card and paid cash for our stay.

Ours was a beautiful, spacious room with a huge, fluffy, four-poster bed. "Is this a little better than the cot?" joked Maurice, who didn't seem nervous at all. Maybe he had more experience than I knew.

It was still light outside, and Maurice began to unbutton his shirt.

"I've never seen you in the daylight," he said. "And I can't wait."

Once he had taken his shirt off, he came over to me and began to slowly unbutton my shirt as he kissed my neck. The sex turned into lovemaking on this fall evening, and we were in our own private world. Our physical contact felt so good and so natural, and we moved together, holding still from time to time and looking into each other's eyes. I did feel a moment of disappointment as I wanted to feel what he was feeling, but lying together afterward was the warmest and closest feeling I had ever had.

"Why didn't I think of this sooner?" Maurice said in his lighthearted, joking way.

"Should I take that as a compliment, Mr. Andrews?" I asked.

He laughed. We both realized today had been a game changer. After just lying together for I don't know how long, Maurice asked, "Shall I draw you a bath, Mrs. Andrews?" My smile was all the answer necessary. He handed me a robe and put one on as he went into the bathroom and started running the water in the tub.

After we bathed together, Maurice put on a gorgeous velvet suit for dinner, and that's when I noticed him dabbing cologne on his neck. Christian Dior's Eau Sauvage! So that was the intoxicating smell I'd been enjoying. I put on my dressy pink mini-dress, this time accompanied by my new black boots from Paris.

"Very nice, Mrs. Andrews. Shall we?" I took his arm as he escorted me from our room.

At the hotel's restaurant, The Little Cottage, we ordered champagne.

Maurice lifted his glass. "To us and our future," he toasted. "I love you."

I was stunned. We had joked about being in love, and Maurice had told me to write my parents that he loved me, but this was different.

"I love you, too," I said as we clinked our glasses together.

I meant it, too. I believed in my heart that I was in love with this man. *So why did I still doubt that this could be real?*

"My wife and I would love to see a menu," Maurice told the waiter.

I hid my giggle behind my glass as I took another sip of champagne. With my newfound appreciation for fish, I ordered sogliola di Dover, fresh Dover sole in a lemon butter sauce. Maurice had veal cordon bleu. We talked and drank our way through a beautiful meal.

All during my visit to England, we'd been discovering one another in so many ways. I'd told him the story of my life, how my parents had instilled confidence in me throughout my life—the very confidence it had taken to get me to this moment with Maurice. In turn, he told me the story of his life: how he and his brothers had always been musically inclined, and how his parents had supported their dreams but never pushed them into show business.

After our entrees arrived, Maurice leaned close and whispered in my ear, "I know what I want for dessert!"

Before retiring for the night, we took a walk in the crisp evening air. We held hands while we window shopped and people-watched. I spotted a beautiful jade necklace in the window of a jewelry store that Maurice agreed would look great on me. He kept making me laugh by making fun of people, though not in a cruel way—joking about a silly hat or some awful outfit someone was wearing. Maurice's comments about Paul McCartney and his girlfriend were the only negative things I ever heard him say about anyone or anything. What would he think, I wondered, if I repeated the bitchy thing Lulu had said to me?

It was pretty chilly outside. “Let’s take a hot bath *before* bed,” Maurice said, smiling, “and then the sheets will feel cool against our skin.” Just the thought of another playful, intimate bath thrilled me.

That night, we fell asleep in each other’s arms.

When I awoke in the morning, my face was just inches from Maurice’s. He was sleeping so peacefully, his hair framing his face. I was overwhelmed to be waking up next to the man I loved. When he awoke, he didn’t speak; he just smiled and pulled me into a passionate kiss. What a way to start the day!

After another round of lovemaking and yet another lovely hot bath, Maurice said, “I’d like to take you out to Kent today. It’s a beautiful village where I was going to buy that farm, and I want to show you. Let’s take your camera.”

I put on the navy pinstriped pantsuit Mom had made especially for this trip, and after tea and toast from room service, we headed out. It was a lovely Sunday, with only a few high clouds. Ironically, at this point in the trip I still hadn’t taken a single picture of myself with Maurice. We were scheduled to do a photo shoot of the Bee Gees the next day, but I felt like he would think I was taking advantage of my position at *Tiger Beat* if I took pictures of the two of us. I’m sure Maurice would have thought that a silly notion, but I was just afraid to bring up the subject. As a result, I have only memories, but no photographs of the two of us on the best trip of my life with my first true love.

The drive to Kent was gorgeous, all rolling green hills and misty hillsides—I definitely wasn't in California anymore. As Maurice drove, we sang along with whatever was on the radio. I remember singing along to the Association's "Never My Love." Well, Maurice sang; I barely whispered, so he wouldn't hear my voice, because I'm incapable of singing on key. And who's going to sing along with a singing superstar?

Unfortunately, at one point Maurice stopped singing, and when he heard me, he began to laugh. "I hope you won't sing to our babies," he joked. "You'll ruin them for life!"

He wasn't being mean—he was right! I laughed as hard as he did. He added, "This is officially 'our song.'" And he sang along:

You ask me if there'll come a time
When I grow tired of you
Never my love
Never my love. . .

Driving through Kent's narrow countryside roads, I'd sometimes lean against Maurice's arm, as it looked like we were going to crash into the high hedges alongside. Every time, he'd laugh and say, "I've got this. There won't be any Bobbies chasing us, I assure you!" referring to my near run-in with the London coppers.

Maurice found a secluded area with wide, open spaces adjacent to a beautiful horse farm. He was intent on capturing me on film, so he took pictures of me with the horses, sitting on a park bench, standing casually against a tree. These became his memory pictures and the only ones for me from the trip.

That night, back in London, we attended a Pink Floyd concert at the Saville Theater. While they put on a great show, I was much more interested in watching Maurice as he watched the band. *That* was my idea of a good evening. After the show, Stiggy asked us to join him for dinner. He seemed to like me, and the three of us had a delightful meal and conversation.

This would be the last night at our hotel, as we had told Maurice's folks we'd be home "from the country" on Monday. We made the most of our private time that night and the next morning. After long, slow, and tender lovemaking, he held me close and sang "our song" softly into my ear: "*You wonder if this heart of mine will lose its desire for you, never my love, never my love.*" His was the sweetest voice I had ever heard. I could barely breathe.

The next day, I was scheduled to photograph the Bee Gees for *Tiger Beat.* We met at Barry's flat, which seemed outdated and under-furnished. The band might have had two worldwide hits, but they weren't rolling in money just yet. I took pictures of them in and around the street where Barry lived. Maurice had dressed for the photo shoot in a wild turquoise-and-red-striped shirt, a brown suede vest with turquoise trim, and the necklace I had made for him—this last detail melted my heart. I told him how much it meant to me, and he, in turn, told me how much he loved wearing the necklace, knowing I had made it especially for him.

I shot color for some full-color *TB* pin-ups, as well as black and white shots we'd use over the coming months. All the guys were just as nice and cooperative as they'd been the first time I met them in Beverly Hills.

The next day, I joined the group at a recording studio, where they were working on their fourth album. I was invited to stay for the entire recording session and had the okay to photograph them as they worked. By now, I'd been to many recording sessions, but this was different because I loved this band's music—and my boyfriend was *in* the band! On this particular day, they were working on a new single, "Words." Maurice told me he had written most of the melodies, while Barry and Robin had written most of the lyrics. He also confided that I was the inspiration for his three new songs, and would be on all those he wrote from then on.

At one point, the guys ran out of paper to write on, so I gave Robin one of my "From Ann Moses, *Tiger Beat Magazine*" printed notepads, and he wrote down the lyrics for them to read as they sang into the microphones. I think we printed a photo of that note in *FaVE!*, but, sadly, I didn't keep the original.

Later that evening, I phoned my friend Teri Pierce in Hollywood. She was house sitting for me, and I wanted to check in with her. I hadn't spoken to her since the week before, when I had called to tell her about how Maurice and I had caught Andy selling Barry's bath water to fans—really the funniest thing I had ever seen!

"Why don't we have her listen to the track we've laid down so far," Maurice suggested, "and get her opinion of it?"

"Great!" I replied. It was 4 a.m. Hollywood time, but Teri began screaming when she realized I was calling all the way from London. I briefly told her how wonderful my weeks had been and explained that we'd been in the recording studio for several hours. Maurice took the receiver and said hello and asked her if she'd tell them what she thought of their new recording. "I want you to be really honest," he said, "and let me know exactly what your thoughts are on this. We need some opinions that aren't ours, since we've been listening to it for hours!"

"The next thing I heard was 'Smile an everlasting smile, a smile could bring you near to me'," Teri remembered. "And of course I *loved* it. Maurice played it again a couple of times so I could really feel it, and I *still* loved it!"

After we got off the phone, the band asked me to make them tea. I didn't have the nerve to admit I had no clue how to make tea, so I nodded cheerfully. Maurice showed me the little kitchen in the studio offices, and I started to heat up a kettle of water. I dug my spoon into the loose tea leaves, but I had *no idea* how much tea to put in. Just as I was about to "wing it" and pray that my concoction was drinkable, an older gentleman came barreling into the kitchen and shouted at me, "What the hell do you think you're doing!?"

"The band wanted tea," I meekly answered.

He grabbed the spoon and carton of tea leaves from my hands and snarled, "*I* am the Tea Master of this studio! It's my job to make tea, and you need to leave *now*!"

I was embarrassed and relieved at the same time. The boys would have their tea break, and it wouldn't wind up a disaster instead of a caffeine boost. We all enjoyed the perfectly brewed tea with biscuits (I thought it was so cute how in Britain, cookies were "biscuits").

We got home at four in the morning and slept until noon, after which Maurice headed back to the studio. I made a final visit to Carnaby Street with Donna, who was anxious to hear all about my sexy adventures with my rock star boyfriend. At dinnertime, we returned to the same Italian restaurant. This time we saved lots of room for Croquembouche.

That night, Maurice and I stayed up talking until 4 a.m. I had so many things on my mind that I didn't get to sleep until 6:30, then got up at 9:30 to pack. I said my thank yous to the Gibbs, who lined up to hug me good-bye. They really seemed to like me, and I felt the same way toward them. As a final surprise, Maurice had arranged to borrow John Lennon's Rolls to take me to the airport. We had tea and toast at the airport before my flight.

By now, we knew Maurice wouldn't be visiting me in Hollywood in November, as we'd planned, because the Bee Gees were booked for an appearance at the Saville Theatre. He told me how much he was going to miss me, and how he'd make every effort to come to Hollywood as soon as he got any kind of break. As he walked me to the departure gate, we shared a beautiful kiss and hug good-bye, and I cried softly, knowing how much I'd miss him—and the two of us together. He wiped the tears from my cheeks and promised, "It won't be long before we're together. Don't forget for a moment that I love you."

"I love you, too," I said. "That's why I can't stop crying. Thank you for the best time of my life. Please come over soon!"

Maurice kissed me again, and I boarded the plane. Once I found my seat, I couldn't help but just sit and weep softly. My heart was full from this life-altering experience. Never having felt so in love, it was only now that I realized the pain of separation.

After three weeks of Maurice's devotion and day after day of exciting new experiences, I'd finally learned to stop wondering how someone as special as Maurice could really love me. My heart believed his love was true.

Chapter 13

Back Home to Hollywood—and Heartbreak

On the plane ride home, I wrote my parents about all the fun we'd had the last few days. "I can't begin to tell you how beautiful everything is with Maurice," I wrote, "like never *ever* before. You're going to love him. He says he already loves you for having me. Isn't that sweet!

"Of course, I haven't gotten one bit of work done," my letter continued. "So, I've got a head full of excuses to give at the office. I hope they aren't too upset. But even if they are, I don't care, because I've had the greatest time of my life. I can't remember being so happy, and I'm ready to go back and work hard now."

When I did return to work at *Tiger Beat*, Ralph and Chuck were more than pleased with the great stories I'd gotten while "on vacation." I wrote up my interview with Davy Jones' friend Basil Foster, the story about my day on the Herman's Hermits movie set, and lots of articles (with photos) on the Bee Gees. I kept the more intimate details of my trip to myself; I wasn't close enough with anyone at the office, other than Teri, to share any details of my love affair with Maurice.

Within a few days, I was back to my routine, though whenever I let my mind wander, I daydreamed about my time with Maurice. Every time "Never My Love" came on the radio, I got huge knots in my stomach. I missed him so much.

I filled my days and nights playing catch-up at work, writing letters to Maurice, and making his birthday present—another Indian bead necklace, this time in colors of red, white, and blue (for both the US flag and the Union Jack). His birthday was December 22, so I needed to send off his gift a few weeks in advance.

In November, I realized I hadn't had a period since I came home. I was at least three weeks late. I'd never missed a period, and I was truly terrified I might be pregnant. I knew as well as anyone that it only takes one stray swimmer to make a baby, and Maurice's "pull out method" was well known to fail. If I was pregnant, what would Maurice do? What would I do? We were in love, but did that mean we were ready for a baby? What if it made him run for the hills and leave me on my own? Would I agree to marry him if I thought he was being forced to "do the right thing"? I didn't think so!

I didn't share my panic with Maurice or anyone. Instead, I went to see Dr. Blood and confided my fears. He did a blood test immediately. The test results wouldn't be back for two days, and those were two of the longest days I've ever lived through.

I wasn't pregnant. Dr. Blood said I had probably missed my period because of all the stress and excitement of the previous weeks. He prescribed the same birth control pills I'd taken the year before, and I nearly collapsed with joy and relief.

My heart was still in London, but I was really busy at work. I resumed all my regular assignments like "I Visit with the Monkees" and my "Meow" column, and there was a whole new group of faves to cover. The Cowsills had just had their first hit record, and I arranged an interview with them so I could introduce the family to *Tiger Beat* readers. For "Meow," I made sure to get a picture of me jumping on their trampoline with Susan Cowsill.

I began making regular trips to the set of *The Flying Nun*, a popular sitcom about a nun who was so skinny, gusts of wind blew her high into the air. Sally Field, the star of the show, had agreed to put her name on a monthly column titled "Be My Friend by Sally Field." I wrote her columns with material from interviews I did with her on the set, between takes. She was such a nice young woman, and her future husband, Steve Craig, was a fraternity brother of my brother Jack at University of Southern California. I enjoyed visiting that set because of all the physical "flying" they did, hauling Sally and her stunt double around on wires. It was fun to see TV magic in action, and the stars of the series really seemed to enjoy making each episode.

Though I still had the title of feature editor, I'd actually been the acting editor-in-chief of *Tiger Beat* for more than a year. I was responsible for all story assignments, layout, copy and art approval, and had final say on everything that went into each issue as well as who was on every cover. I was paid an editor's wages, but I didn't have the official title.

To everyone who saw me, I was still Annie Moses, feature editor of *Tiger Beat*. But I felt like a completely different girl since my trip to London. Maurice called several times a week, and each time I heard his voice, it was like we were together again. He'd finally figured out how to call me when it was daytime or evening in California, and not at 4 or 5 a.m. He always was eager to know what I was doing, and he told me about appearances the Bee Gees had made. He was still looking for a place of his own in the country, with a separate house on the property for his parents and grandmother.

I began counting the days until Maurice and his brothers would arrive in LA at the end of January 1968. They'd be performing live and taping an appearance on the wildly popular *Smothers Brothers Comedy Hour*. We were both giddy with excitement, knowing we'd be together again.

I'd been planning my Christmas present for Maurice since the day I'd arrived home. I was a pretty good seamstress; as a kid, my mom had paid me ten cents an hour to do handwork like basting seams and stitching jacket collars. I asked her, "If I do the handwork, will you make an original jacket for Maurice for Christmas?"

Mom agreed. She'd never seen her daughter so happy, and she would have done anything for Maurice.

With just such a gift in mind, I'd purchased some incredibly psychedelic brocade suit fabric from one of the hippest shops on Carnaby Street. While I was staying in his room in London, I had taken the measurements of one of Maurice's jackets. With only weeks before Christmas, Mom and I worked every weekend until the fantastic, one-of-a-kind jacket was done. As I'd done many times before, I drove her into Hollywood to a special store across the street from the famous Farmers Market, where we found some unique brass buttons that were perfect against the brocade. I carefully packaged the jacket and sent it air mail to arrive just in time for Christmas. My card said, "I hope this gift blows your mind, like you blow my mind! Merry Christmas, All My Love, Annie."

A few days before Christmas, a package arrived from London. As I had in years past, I was going to spend Christmas Eve and Christmas Day with my family at my parents' house. I put the package in my car along with my overnight bag when I drove down on Christmas Eve morning.

I woke up before my parents on Christmas morning and sat with the wrapped present in my hand as I sipped a cup of tea. *Finally,* my parents got up, and my brother, his wife and son arrived to open gifts. Everyone wanted me to go first. I opened the beautiful card, in which Maurice had written, "You are my inspiration. You said this was your favorite, so I hope my favorite girl likes this, too. Happy Christmas, Love, Maurice." I opened the small box as his note was passed around the living room. Inside the velvet jewelry box was the gorgeous jade pendant necklace we had seen in the jewelry shop window just weeks ago. No hippie love beads, but an exquisite gift with my favorite stone, beautiful green jade. I loved it.

Maurice and I talked on the phone the next day, both of us gushing over our gifts from one another. He couldn't believe the jacket my mom and I had made for him, and said his brothers were very jealous. I told him I'd never received such a loving and thoughtful gift as my jade necklace. We were both counting the days until he arrived in Hollywood.

The weeks before the Bee Gees returned to Hollywood were a blur. Maurice called me the minute he got to the Beverly Hills Hotel, and I met them at CBS Television Studios for their first day of rehearsals for *The Smothers Brothers Comedy Hour.* Afterward, Maurice and I had dinner out, then went "home" to my house. This would be our wonderful routine for the next week and a half. We both were anxious to rekindle the passion of our stay at the Thistle Piccadilly Hotel.

I confided in Maurice about my pregnancy scare, and I told him I was on birth control. When we made love this time, we didn't have to rely on Maurice's "pulling out" routine—and what a difference it made! *So, this was what they meant about fireworks and the earth moving!* An even more likely explanation was my growing sense of security that I was truly loved, because Maurice had been so actively pursuing me with letters, phone calls, and his beautiful Christmas gift. What's more, he had chosen to spend the entire week at my house rather than be with his brothers at the Beverly Hills Hotel.

We made love every night and every morning after waking up together. It was bliss. We were in America—equipped with showers, not just bathtubs as in England—so each morning we enjoyed showering together, then I'd make us tea with milk and sugar before we'd head out for the day. I cheated with tea bags, but it was English Breakfast Tea, not Lipton.

We spent the next two days at CBS. I'd made arrangements with the press department to have full access to the Smothers Brothers rehearsals, and I sat in the empty audience seats, taking lots of great pictures. Each time they took a break, Maurice was by my side. On Friday night, the show, which would air on the night after my twenty-first birthday, was taped before a live audience. It was spectacular. The Bee Gees performed "Words," their new hit, which I'd watched them record a few months before.

The next night, the Bee Gees headlined their first American concert at the Anaheim Convention Center. More than 9,000 tickets were sold, and the guys were paid $50,000—$5000 more than the Beatles received per night for their two appearances at the Hollywood Bowl in 1965.

No need for a backstage pass at this concert—Stiggy was kind enough to let me ride down with the boys in their limousine. I got some great shots of them onstage and backstage as well. The trip home was exciting because they were all so thrilled at the massive, enthusiastic reception they received. This had been their biggest audience to date.

When we woke up late Sunday morning—or was it afternoon?—Maurice and I had the whole day to ourselves. It was a perfect California day, so we took a drive up Pacific Coast Highway to Malibu. We walked along the shore just north of Malibu and waded in the cold Pacific, hand in hand. We were never at a loss for words. In this romantic setting, Maurice would often stop, pull me into his arms, and plant a passionate kiss on my lips. "You are so beautiful," he told me.

That night, back at home, I made the only real dinner I knew how to cook: pork chops baked with apples and raisins, with rice pilaf on the side. I wasn't twenty-one yet, but I had a friend buy us a bottle of champagne to remind us of our dinner at The Little Cottage. Maurice praised my cooking, which made me feel fantastic.

I'd told the folks at *Tiger Beat* I wouldn't be in much that week. They thought it was because I was focused on covering the Bee Gees' two weeks in Hollywood, but word got around that Maurice and I were dating. At work, only Teri knew how serious our romance had become.

Our time together was idyllic. We joined the Bee Gees at the Hollywood premier of the John Lennon and Michael Crawford movie *How I Won the War* and went swimming at the Beverly Hills Hotel. One day, I took the group to Disneyland on free passes I had scored from one of my old supervisors there.

They were like little boys, discovering the magic of the park. I felt like a kid, too: Maurice and I did our share of making out on some of the darker rides.

The night before my birthday, Nancy Sinatra's producer, Lee Hazelwood, threw a party at his beautiful Spanish style home in the San Fernando Valley. Maurice and I attended together, and I knew many of the guests: Davy Jones, Micky Dolenz, his future wife Samantha Juste, Angela Cartwright, and Tommy Smothers. Buddy Rich and Keely Smith were there, as well as an all-girl group that Lee Hazelwood produced called Honey, Ltd. It was a fantastic party, and one of my favorite photos of Maurice and me was taken that night.

We got home late, and made love as we had every other night. Afterward, as we lay in bed in the afterglow, Maurice turned on his side, propped up on one elbow, and said, "I have something to tell you."

He was so serious—more serious than I'd ever seen him before. My stomach knotted with fear.

"What is it?"

"Lulu and I are married."

And then there was silence.

My mind raced: *When? Where? How? Why? How could you spend every minute with me, make love to me every day when you were married? I would never sleep with a married man!*

I was paralyzed. I didn't know what to do. I didn't cry. I couldn't speak.

Eventually, I managed to pull my thoughts together enough to say, "Tomorrow is my twenty-first birthday. You know my parents are having a party here at the house with all my longtime friends from Anaheim. Then Chuck Laufer is having cocktails and dessert at Ralph Benner's house for all my Hollywood friends and my co-workers from *Tiger Beat*. I expect you to be here at 6 p.m. with a limo and flowers."

And then I got out of bed.

"I'll take you to your hotel now," I said, as calmly as I could.

Maurice looked so ashamed. He didn't seem to know what to say either. He didn't try to make excuses, which was wise of him—I wouldn't have believed anything he said, anyway.

We dressed, and he gathered up his things. We drove to the hotel in silence.

As Maurice climbed out of my car, I asked him, "Will you do what I've asked you to do, tomorrow?"

"Yes," he said. He didn't look me in the eye before turning to walk up the path to the bungalow where the band was staying.

Once I was back on Sunset Boulevard, I began to sob. I probably should have pulled over; I couldn't see anything through my tears.

What did I do to deserve such horrible treatment? How could he betray me by telling me he loved me, when he's already married to Lulu?

As I got closer to home, my tears subsided. I told myself, *I'm fine. I will be fine. No one has to know what a fool I've been for believing he loved me.*

But once I was home, I fell apart. I kept replaying Maurice's crushing words in my mind. I ran upstairs to the bathroom, broke out in a cold sweat, and vomited until my stomach was empty. I fell to the floor, unable to get up to crawl into bed. I lay curled in a fetal position on the bathroom rug. After a while, I was cold, and I pulled myself up, washed out my mouth, and staggered to my bed. I fell into a fitful sleep and dreamed of Maurice and me, stepping out of the church on our wedding day. But then I noticed that the woman in the bridal gown had a shock of red hair, and Lulu's face appeared. I jumped up, wide awake and covered in sweat again.

The next morning, I felt as if I hadn't slept a wink. As I sipped my cup of tea, I became nauseated again. *What if he doesn't show up tonight? I'll be alone on my twenty-first birthday. Everyone is expecting Maurice by my side. For whatever reason, he has chosen Lulu as his true love, but if he'll just get me through tonight, I can pick myself up and get back to my life. I have guts. If I resolve to make it on my own, I will make it!*

I certainly hadn't told *anyone* about Maurice's revelations of the night before. My parents had been planning this big celebration for weeks. They had invited my high school friends, my brother and his wife. Mom and Dad weren't in a position to pay for a fancy catered party, so Mom was planning to serve a honey-baked ham, her homemade sweet-and-hot mustard, crescent rolls, and potato salad. They'd bought Korbel champagne, the best within their budget.

Promptly at 6 p.m., the limousine pulled up in front of my Beachwood Drive house. I didn't know whether to laugh, jump with joy, or cry. I gathered up every ounce of my courage: It was show time.

Maurice proved a worthy co-star in our little let's-don't-disappoint-the-party-guests act. He arrived carrying two dozen red roses, kissed me tenderly, and said, "Happy birthday, luv." He looked so handsome in a maroon velvet Edwardian jacket, shiny gray slacks, and a white turtleneck sweater. I introduced him to my parents, and he stayed by my side as other guests arrived, chatting with all my friends, who were more than a little star-struck. But Maurice mingled with everyone, not playing "star" for even a minute. I played my part, as well—at least when anyone was looking. The rest of the time, especially during the few moments we were alone together, I didn't bother to hide my anger and hurt. I was sarcastic, even downright mean to him. *As mean as he's been to me,* I told myself.

Before dinner, my dad offered a lovely toast. "To my beautiful little girl. I was so happy the day you were born! Happy birthday!" Everyone echoed "Happy birthday!" and we dove into our meal. Maurice and I sat together, eating from plastic plates. He complimented my mom on the food, and a couple of hours later, the party broke up. My guests knew I was expected for cocktails and cake at the cocktail party at Ralph's house. Maurice and I rode to Ralph's house in the limo.

Once there, we were greeted with noisy applause. Maurice continued to be attentive to me as we made the rounds, talking to everyone there. While we were busy pretending to be happy, Chuck asked everyone to raise their glasses in a toast.

"When Annie first came into Ralph's office at *Tiger Beat*," he said, "we had just published our fifth issue. It was just Ralph, Laudy, and me putting out the magazine, and in comes this eighteen-year-old girl with the energy and spark of a firecracker. Little did we know that in addition to her winning personality, she would be an outstanding reporter and editor. Since she came on board, *Tiger Beat* has quadrupled its circulation. It is my honor on this very special occasion to announce that Ann Moses is the new editor-in-chief of *Tiger Beat*!"

I have never cried easily in front of people, but I was so overwhelmed that tears filled my eyes. I gave Chuck a big hug, and then I hugged Ralph.

I was in shock. I'd had no idea any of this was in the works, let alone that Chuck would announce it in such a public way. I was proud, and felt momentarily vindicated, as if my new title could soothe the pain of Maurice's devastating betrayal of the night before.

As we said good night to the party guests, I worked overtime to hide my heartbreak. My friends saw a happy young woman who'd just celebrated a milestone birthday, been given a high-profile promotion at work, and had a rock star boyfriend. None of them would have ever guessed that I was devastated, and none of us knew that this was the last time I'd see Maurice in person for the rest of my life.

The limo delivered us to my house, and Maurice walked me to the door. "I'm so sorry," he said again, not meeting my eyes. "Can I kiss you good night?"

He was not just kissing me good night, I realized. He was kissing me good-bye forever. I couldn't resist one last kiss. It was long and sweet, but as the tears started to well in my eyes, I stepped back from his embrace.

Once inside, I sank to the floor, and the tears began to flow. I didn't look out the door to watch Maurice leave. I wanted my last memory of him to be the sorrow I'd seen in his eyes. I'd also seen real love and affection there.

Why had he given his love away?

Chapter 14

How Can You Mend a Broken Heart?

I spent Sunday alone and miserable. I couldn't eat. I was exhausted, but I couldn't sleep. I felt like a complete fool, and I felt used, and that had led to this horrible feeling of emptiness I'd never felt before. When would it go away? Days? Weeks? Months? I had never lost a loved one. No one in my family had died, and this loss felt like a death.

I had never been so grateful to have a job in my life. On Monday morning, I wasn't ready to share what had happened to me. I talked instead about the fun we'd all had at Ralph's party. I continued to receive congratulations on being named editor. Although I'd been the acting editor for more than a year, having the title really meant something special.

After that first day, I coped with my pain and grief by getting myself out of the office all day, every day, so I wouldn't have to answer questions from co-workers and friends. When I told Ralph or Chuck, "I'm off to the *Monkees* set," it was music to their ears. They didn't want me in the office, even though I needed to be there to plan each issue, decide on layout placement, approve the artists' work, and write many stories for each issue. They seemed happiest when they wouldn't see me until the next day or the day after, because it meant I was out reporting first-hand news on the faves.

I never took advantage of their trust. I really did go out in the field, to the set of *Where the Action Is* to interview its guest stars, or out to the Columbia Ranch to talk with Sally Field between scenes of *The Flying Nun*. I was never home before 5 p.m. on any day.

Keeping myself busy worked. It certainly helped that the cutest, most popular guys in the world were my friends. Two days after the breakup, I walked onto the *Monkees* soundstage to find Davy and Peter sitting with a couple of their friends in director's chairs. Davy waved me over, and I sat down and said a quiet "hello."

Immediately, Davy took me by the hand and led me to his dressing room. Once we were alone, he put his hands on my shoulders and looked into my eyes. "What's wrong?" he asked. "I can tell you're really upset."

I had not allowed myself to cry over Maurice. But when Davy asked what was wrong, I couldn't keep the tears back any longer. I told him my boyfriend had broken up with me, and he drew me into a hug as I sobbed on his shoulder.

After a couple of minutes, I composed myself, and Davy sat down beside me. "I don't know who the bastard is," he said. "But *he's* the loser, not you. You are a beautiful lady, and someday you will find the man that's worthy of you."

Hearing Davy's sincere, big-brotherly words lifted my spirits just a little. Later, when I thought back on how he had been worried about *my* feelings, it helped my heart heal a little more.

Time with friends really helped. That week, I went to see the Hollies perform at the Whisky A Go Go, and after their wonderful performance, Bernie Calvert, their bass player, took me out to dinner. A few nights later, I visited Genie the Tailor's house in Laurel Canyon for a heart-to-heart talk. Genie had had her share of love affairs—good and bad—so I confided in her about what had happened.

"Let it go," was her simple advice for me. And, being the true friend she was, she ended with, "You are *way* too good for that asshole."

Genie was persistent. She told me that all the bad things she'd endured had served to make her a better person. She tried to share how I needed to turn this into a personal enrichment experience. But in my heart, I still loved Maurice. How could I "let it go" when I had never been treated with such tenderness, love, and thoughtfulness? If Maurice wasn't my dream come true, it was only because I had never imagined, in my wildest dreams, how feeling truly loved could make me feel.

Still, I trusted Genie, and tried my best to take her words to heart. I slipped back into my "poor me" routine from time to time, but then I'd remember her advice and start trying to turn my pain into something worthwhile.

Two days after my pep talk from Genie, I had lunch with Teri Pierce, who had house sat for me while I was in London and who worked in the *Tiger Beat* mailroom as well as part-time for Beverly Noga, owner of one of Hollywood's top public relations firms. Beverly was Stiggy's publicist and had set up my original interview with the Bee Gees. At lunch, Teri was dying to hear all about my birthday night. All I could say was, "Maurice and I aren't together any more."

"What are you talking about?" she yelped. "You two are in love!"

"He told me he's married to Lulu." I couldn't stop the tears from rolling down my face.

"I can't believe it!" was all she could say.

Two days later, Teri showed up at my house. "I've got some news for you," she said. "Lulu and Maurice *aren't* married!"

I shook my head in astonishment. "How do you know?" I didn't believe her.

Teri had talked to Beverly, who had no idea I'd dated Maurice, about his marriage to Lulu. "And she just laughed!" Teri told me.

Beverly had told Teri that Robert Stigwood was always trying to make "power couples" out of his eligible young clients. She rolled her eyes about how Stiggy had tried to set up Eric Clapton and singer P.P. Arnold as a super couple, and, according to Beverly, Eric had told Stiggy to go fuck himself.

Beverly had heard that Maurice had dated Lulu a few times in November and December 1967, and she had told Teri that Lulu had agreed to do concert dates and TV appearances with the Bee Gees if Stiggy could convince Maurice to continue dating her. Stiggy was also sending Barry Gibb out on dates with Stiggy's female clients to create buzz on them in the press; meanwhile, Barry's live-in girlfriend was a deep, dark secret.

Teri had also learned from Beverly that while Maurice was spending time with me in Hollywood, he had received explicit instructions from Stiggy to break it off with me, lest any of Stiggy's publicity "deals" be ruined. I imagine that Maurice's "confession" to me had been scripted by Stiggy, who hoped I wouldn't fight for a married man's love or become some kind of betrayed lover who would stalk his client. I imagine, too, that Maurice's appearance at my parties was his way of being kind to me. I've always believed he was a good person but, young and perched on the edge of super-stardom, was maybe too afraid to stand up for himself. He had his brothers to think of, and their manager was calling the shots. It can't have been an easy decision for him. Could it?

I was in an awkward position myself. As the editor of a popular magazine about singing stars, I had to think of others, too. When Beverly asked me to run a publicity piece on Lulu, I created a glowing, two-page spread in the March 1968 *Tiger Beat*. Likewise, I continued to print stories on the Bee Gees, who were becoming more popular. In that same March issue, I ran a piece titled "The Bee Gees' Secret Recording Session," illustrated with all the photos I had taken in the London studio as they recorded "Words." In the May issue, I ran photos taken at the Lee Hazelwood party that Maurice and I had attended the night before my birthday party. Later that year, I even printed that Maurice had attended Lulu's opening at a club in London, based on a press release from Beverly's office.

I couldn't seem to get away from Lulu. She was huge in the UK and was catching on in America, too. When she opened for the Monkees during their summer tour of London, I'd written about her and Davy "dating," even though I knew he lived with his girlfriend, with whom I was friendly. When Lulu came to Hollywood in 1968 to play the Coconut Grove nightclub, Davy asked me to come and take pictures of him and Lulu together. Although it was gut-wrenching to be near her, I did as Davy asked—mostly because I knew I could sell the photos to *New Musical Express.*

As I drove to meet them outside the Ambassador Hotel, I began to regret having agreed to this favor. I didn't want to photograph Lulu—I wanted to scratch her eyes out. I worried she might gloat about dating Maurice, but she never mentioned him. I said, "Hi," like I was meeting a longtime friend, and Lulu acted as if nothing had ever transpired between us. She was totally in the moment: She and Davy hugged and kissed for my camera, Lulu playing the role of the star with her name on the marquee, and I was the lowly reporter/photographer coming to get a story. I made small talk, she thanked me, and we were done. As I drove home, I felt relieved this encounter was behind me.

What I didn't know then was that Maurice and Lulu had broken up after dating for several months. Teri, who'd left *Tiger Beat* and was working full-time for Beverly, wrote press releases for all of Stiggy's clients, including the Bee Gees. During a trip to Hollywood several months after we had broken up, Maurice stopped in at Beverly's office.

"I reminded him we had sort of met when you and he had called me from the recording studio to get my opinion on the song they were recording," Teri told me. She said Maurice had looked shocked, but that he remembered that night well. He was also shocked when Teri asked him, "Are you still seeing the skank?"

"You mean Lulu?" he asked innocently.

"Yeah, the skank you left Annie for," Teri replied. She told me he hung his head and admitted, "We broke up."

Teri said Maurice began to quiz her. "Do you still talk to Annie? How is she? How does she look? Is she dating anyone?"

Teri said she had told him I was dating a friend from high school, but that it wasn't serious. She remembered asking Maurice, "Why don't you call her?"

"That's not a good idea," he told her. "I think she hates me. I didn't leave on good terms. It was my fault. I was mean to her, and too much time has gone by. But I'll never forget her."

Teri said to Maurice, “I thought you two were in love. Was I wrong?”

He answered her: “Annie was very playful, funny, and she had a beautiful heart.” Teri added, “He told me the thing that impressed him more than anything is that you never said no to him.”

For the next year, Teri worked with the Bee Gees on their United States public relations, and she got to know Maurice well. During that time, she said, whenever Maurice was in Hollywood, Lulu called Teri’s office constantly.

“What’s he doing today?” Lulu would ask. “What interviews are they doing? Which magazines?” Out of spite, Teri told me one day she answered, “They’ve got an interview with *Tiger Beat* this afternoon.” She said the line fell silent.

Teri had fibbed, but she was fed up with the constant calls from Lulu. Teri also told me that every time Lulu called, Maurice tried to dodge her. “Tell her I’m not here,” he often told Teri.

Lulu and Maurice weren’t even dating at the time, although she was still after him, still pressing Stiggy to use his influence to get them back together.

It worked. By November 1968, they were dating again. Two months later, I received a press release saying the couple was engaged, and I printed the news in my March 1969 “Meow” column. By this time, I had moved on. Maurice and Lulu were married in February of that year, and I printed the wedding picture in the May issue.

(In a 2010 *Daily Mail* article, Lulu talked about her marriage to Maurice, claiming they had met "when we both appeared on *Top of the Pops*. I was twenty when we married. We were far too young. We were two spoiled little pop stars, each too used to having our own way. The problem was, our life was one long party, and it became too much for me. I loved my career, but I wanted a normal life, too.")

Genie was right: Tragedy could be used in a positive way. I had stopped thinking about "what ifs." I had learned to pour myself into my work. And I never again "fell for" any of the other stars I wrote about. Instead, I created friendships and working relationships with celebrities and kept my own life outside of show business. I kept telling myself I was bent, not broken.

During this time, while I was still mourning the loss of what I thought of as my first true love, I began dating my high school friend Don, whom I hadn't seen since he left for Vietnam two years earlier. He lived with his parents in Anaheim, and he'd come to my house on the weekends to hang out. While it was not any kind of real courtship, the two of us found comfort in one another. There was no romance to speak of, but at that point I was hungry for validation that *anyone* would ever care about me or love me. I thought Don was an excellent lover, but at my young age I didn't know much about passion versus sex. We had little else to bond us together. Nonetheless, in the spring of 1969, I proposed to him.

Did I think Don was my soul mate, my forever love? Not really. Looking back, I'm sure I was just seeking the security I thought came with being married. We never discussed our dreams for the future, except for one thing: Don made it clear early on that he never wanted what he called "rug rats" or "curtain climbers." At the time, not having children didn't strike me as a problem.

We were married in July in St. Michael's Episcopal Church in Anaheim. It was a small wedding, with a dozen or so guests. My mom cooked all the food for the reception, which was held in my parents' back yard. We didn't go on a honeymoon, because four days after the wedding we were headed to Vegas to see Elvis' first concert appearance there.

I see now that I settled for the safer path of marriage, something many women my age did at the time, despite the changes beginning to happen in our society.

My marriage set the stage for the next few years. The Ann Moses who was a self-assured go-getter, whose boss had once described her as a "girl with the energy and spark of a firecracker," gradually faded into the background.

Chapter 15

The King and I

My love affair with Elvis began in 1956. I was nine years old, and my friends and I had been dancing to his records at our fifth-grade garage parties for quite some time when he made his first appearance on *The Milton Berle Show*. It wasn't his first television appearance, but it was the first one I'd seen. He sang "Hound Dog," and that's all it took. I became a true Elvis fan on June 5, 1956.

Unlike the Catholics and the Southern Baptists who were outraged by his onstage bumping and grinding and gyrations, my parents weren't afraid their pre-teen children were going to be "ruined" by listening to this rock singer.

Their acceptance only went so far, though. I was supremely disappointed that Christmas when I didn't receive the Elvis Presley felt skirt (like a poodle skirt, but with a silhouette of Elvis' face where the poodle would be) I'd asked for—although Santa did leave an Elvis scarf under our tree. My love affair lasted another year or two, but by 1959 Elvis was sharing my love with James Darren (from the first *Gidget* movie with Sandra Dee) and other popular singers. Mom allowed me to cut their pictures out of movie magazines and tape them to the closet doors in my room, and my folks let me buy 45s, as long as I played them in my room with the door shut. By 1960, I'd switched to Top 40 radio, and my love affair with Elvis was over. I didn't go to his movies or pay attention to his life, although it was hard to miss that infamous *Life* magazine article about the haircut he got before being inducted into the Army. Unlike his diehard fans, I didn't shed a tear when he shipped out to Germany.

During the next six years, my life was filled with junior high and high school activities like working on the yearbook and trying to make decent grades. I had a full social life of dances, high school sporting events, and an occasional boyfriend. And like so many young people my age, once the British Invasion had hit America in early 1964, my personal taste in music ran to groups like the Beatles, the Rolling Stones, the Dave Clark Five, and Herman's Hermits. During this same time, Elvis was making the worst movies of his career. I frankly lost interest in the King.

He resurfaced in my life after I went to work for *Tiger Beat* in 1966. I learned that the old cliché is true, especially in Hollywood: It's not *what* you know, but *who* you know. Graylon Landon, head of publicity for RCA Records, was one among many publicists who called me about plugging their artists in *TB*. Graylon had to promote the soundtrack albums turned out by Elvis for each of the pitiful movies his manager, Colonel Tom Parker, forced Elvis to make.

Graylon always sent me tickets to these awful movies, but I'd give them to my friends Tony and Don, who were absolute Elvis nuts—until I became aware of the huge demand for everything Elvis in Europe and the UK. After that, I began attending the films myself and wrote reviews of them for *New Musical Express*.

I rediscovered Elvis while I was covering him for *NME*, and I warmed to his new persona as a grown-up star of the 1960s and 70s. In one of my "America Calling" columns, I wrote: "If the Elvis fans in England were as disappointed with *Speedway* as I was, all I can say is, be patient! Last week I attended a sneak preview of *Live a Little, Love a Little*, Elvis' latest film due for November release. You won't believe what you see! Elvis looks about 21 years old, very slender with groovy new sideburns. His clothes are almost mod and look fantastic. For the first time, he plays a grown man and the feminine lead is played a by a woman, instead of a girl. The songs (which are excellent) blend smoothly with the story line, which is original and very, very funny."

I continued to do publicity favors for Graylon, such as interviews with up-and-coming RCA stars like Harry Nilsson. I'm still kicking myself about the time I sent a *Tiger Beat* editorial assistant to interview a new singer RCA had just signed and whom Graylon was promoting. That singer was John

Denver, and years later I became a devoted fan who had blown her chance to meet a great talent.

The next time Graylon called me, in June of 1968, he had a pair of tickets to a top-secret television taping he said he knew I would enjoy. *Whatever*, I thought. *You scratch my back, I'll scratch yours.*

Graylon had already treated me to a tour of Elvis' and Col. Parker's office at MGM Studios. I'd never seen anything like it in my life: Every square inch of the walls and ceilings was covered with pictures of Elvis, movie posters, and concert posters. The office was like an Elvis shrine, taken to the extreme. That day, I met some of the Memphis Mafia: Charlie Hodge, Joe Esposito, and Richard Davis, Elvis' stand-in in all his films. I tried to get Richard to book an interview with me, but his answer was a firm "no." He didn't do interviews about his friend Elvis.

This time, Graylon had tickets for the taping of *Elvis*, the TV show fans usually refer to as "the 1968 Comeback Special." It was his first television special in eight years, and he'd been rehearsing for two weeks at the NBC studios in Burbank. By June 27, 1968, the second-to-last night of taping, the cameras had captured more than forty hours of tape, which would be edited into a one-hour special to air in December. Graylon had two seats for me at the final taping. I didn't have to be asked twice!

Because I wasn't covering this second night of taping as a member of the press, I waited outside the studio for over two hours with all the other ticket holders while Elvis and his crew rehearsed. There were about 200 of us, and once we were inside and seated around the fifteen-foot-square stage, Elvis' wife, Priscilla, came in with some friends and sat right behind me. The pictures I had seen of her made her look rather hard, but in person she was petite and lovely. Her beehive hairdo was gone, and her hair hung softly on her shoulders. She was wearing a simple black and white dress.

After a while, a producer came out and explained that for this next sequence, he needed people to sit on the steps surrounding the platform. Hands darted up all around the audience, but he said he'd choose the people he wanted. I couldn't believe my good fortune—I was one of the lucky ones chosen to sit on the steps!

After we were seated, an announcer yelled, "Ladies and gentlemen...Mr. Elvis Presley!"

It was like turning the clock back ten years. There stood Elvis, the legend and the man, slimmer than I had seen him in his past few movies. Dressed from head to toe in black leather, his coal-black hair combed back thick and shiny, his skin smooth with only a touch of make-up, he stepped onto the platform, grabbed the guitar from his friend, Lance LeGault, and read the first line on the cue card in front of him: "Well, I'm gonna have to do this sooner or later, so here goes..."

Then he smiled, curled his lip into a sneer as only he could do, planted his feet far apart, and blasted straight into the first verse of "Hound Dog."

From there he sang "Blue Suede Shoes," "Don't Be Cruel," "Heartbreak Hotel," and "Jailhouse Rock." In between numbers, he'd walk around the platform, smile at one of us below, or move into a different pose.

His presence was indescribable. It had been eight years since Elvis had performed these songs live, yet every twist, every hip grind was so precise, you felt the impact. As I watched him perform, I realized he was very aware of the power he possessed. He knew how to look sexy or cruel or tender, and sometimes I'd catch the slightest smile playing across his lips, suggesting he also knew he still had the power to enthrall an audience.

This audience was made up of old women, grown men, and teenagers alike, and all of them were freaking out over The King. I noticed the guys were just as eager to touch and get near Elvis as the women were.

In the edited version of this sequence, as Elvis sings my all-time-favorite song, "Can't Help Falling in Love," my face is superimposed over Elvis' as he's singing. On the night this special aired, I took photos of this shot, with my face on top of Elvis's, right off the television screen. I still loved all the British groups, but I became an Elvis fan all over again, that night.

After *Elvis* aired, I had constant requests for any and all news on the King from my editor at *NME* and a fan magazine in

England called *Elvis Monthly*. I knew Elvis was making a new movie, *Change of Habit*, so I called Graylon to pull some strings. I knew Elvis never did personal interviews, and that no one from the press was allowed on his movie sets. But Graylon put me in touch with the film's unit publicist, Walter Burrell, who agreed to let me "watch" filming of *Change of Habit*. I was not to approach Elvis or any other actor in the movie, and, of course, I wasn't to take any photographs. I was also told not to take notes; I should just hang at the back of the set and observe. I agreed. Even with all the restrictions, I was still thrilled to get to watch Elvis make a movie. It certainly never occurred to me that I'd meet him face to face.

As I wrote in *NME*:

"Mary Tyler Moore, of the Dick Van Dyke TV comedy series, is Elvis's leading lady in the film. When I arrived, she was having her makeup checked, then it happened...all of a sudden there he was, his dark black hair blowing freely in the slight breeze!"

My story went on: "Between shots, Elvis hugged and kissed Mary Tyler Moore, then retreated to his high set chair, where he talked with his buddies, who are always close by, then he'd have a swig of bottled water, which is all he drinks, or sit and puff on a mini-cigar."

I didn't write about something I observed that day, something that struck me as one of the oddest things I'd ever seen. Between shots, Elvis—who was married to Priscilla and had a baby daughter, Lisa Marie—and Mary Tyler Moore, who was married to television producer Grant Tinker, would lie on a big blanket out in the sunshine of the park, surrounded by extras and other actors, making out like teenagers. I don't mean affectionate pecks on the lips, either. I'm talking about arms wrapped around each other during lip-locks that lasted fifteen minutes or half an hour. No one else on the set paid any attention to this behavior from the film's two stars, either out of politeness or because it was somehow commonplace to them. For me, it was very uncomfortable seeing these two married grown-ups behaving like lustful teenagers. I don't think it had anything to do with staying in character, either, because Mary Tyler Moore played a nun in the movie, so they weren't exactly practicing love scenes. Perhaps this happened on every movie set, I reasoned. Maybe it was a side of Hollywood I'd never experienced before.

An Elvis Presley set was a very strange place in other ways, as well. For one thing, hardly anyone spoke to or approached Elvis when he wasn't working, which had to have been arranged in advance, somehow. The other thing was that everyone on this film set seemed to be so happy. Even when things didn't run as smoothly as everyone might have liked, Elvis told jokes, clowned with Mary Tyler Moore, or burst into song to keep a smile on everyone's face. I had been to other TV and movie sets, and things were often tense when filming was delayed by a technical problem or a tardy actor. Elvis' set seemed more like a big, relaxed party.

Occasionally, Elvis glanced over at me with a curious look on his face. No one was allowed to visit Elvis on the set without permission from his longtime manager, Col. Parker, and since Elvis didn't know me, I'm sure he couldn't figure out why I was there.

Still, each time he looked in my direction, there I'd be, staring straight into his eyes. He did wink at me once, though. That was nice.

I got invited back to the studio on Monday to watch another day of shooting. When I arrived, Elvis was already on an indoor set, lip-synching to a recording of "Rubberneckin'," a rousing song from the film. Most of the morning was taken up filming this song from every angle—first the whole scene, then a profile, then a close-up, then a shot of his hands playing the guitar, and so on. I probably heard "Rubberneckin'" about fifteen times that day.

Later, during a break, Elvis slipped into a dark suede jacket and sat at the back of the soundstage. Walter, wonderful Walter, walked over and spoke to Elvis.

The next thing I knew, Elvis was standing in front of me, his dark hair falling to the tops of his eyebrows, his deep blue eyes smiling at me. Butterflies fluttered madly in my stomach.

"Ann Moses," Walter started, "I'd like you to meet Elvis Presley."

It was both formal and still casual, all at the same time. Elvis shook my hand, and I think I muttered, "How do you do?" It was very strange, but at that very moment, all my fears were gone. He put me at complete ease.

"Walter told me all I was allowed to do is watch you," I said. "I've been watching you *real hard.* I hope it hasn't bugged you."

"Not at all," he said. Then he smiled that smile.

"That song is really great," I said. "Did you see Walter and Jane dancing back there?"

"Yeah. Weren't they great? I really dig it when people react when I'm singing—I just get more excited!" He paused. "Look at my fingers," he said as he held out his hands to me. He'd been playing the guitar for nearly four hours that morning, and the calluses had tiny cuts all over them. Before I could react, he touched my arm and excused himself, as he was being called to do another shot. A few minutes later, he returned to continue our conversation.

"Did you have your jacket specially made?" I asked. "It's great-looking."

"You know, I found it on the rack," he said. "That happens every once in a while. I was pretty lucky."

"I guess Vegas is next."

He muttered, "Yep!"

"I was at the taping of your TV special," I continued, but Elvis broke in.

"*That's* where I've seen you! Your face looked so familiar to me these past two days, but I couldn't figure out where I'd seen you."

"Our faces are superimposed on the screen for a few seconds while you sing 'Can't Help Falling in Love,'" I said.

"That must be it! I *knew* you looked familiar." Before he could go on, he was called back to the set. Sadly, Walter was already late for another appointment, and I was there as his guest. We rushed off—no time for goodbyes, no thank yous.

I'd met Elvis, and he had remembered me. I didn't imagine anything could be quite so exciting as that, but the next morning I received a letter from the publicist at the International Hotel in Las Vegas, informing me that my seat had been reserved for Elvis' opening there in July.

Would we meet again? I could only hope!

Chapter 16

Here Comes Bobby Sherman

Even though Bobby Sherman was a regular on the pop music variety show *Shindig* from September 1964 through January 1966, I never saw him perform during that time. Like most families, we had one television in the living room. My dad chose what programs we watched in the evening, and he loved Westerns. *Shindig* aired opposite *Daniel Boone* on Thursday nights, so *Daniel Boone* it was.

My first exposure to this talented guy came when we previewed some of the TV shows set to premier in the fall of 1968. Bobby appeared in the October *Tiger Beat* that year, in an article titled "Here They Are: TV's Brightest New Stars and Shows." The story introduced Peter Kastner, who'd be playing a cross-dressing role as a female model in *The Ugliest Girl in Town*, and mentioned Lucille Ball's new show, *Here's Lucy*, which would co-star *TB* fave Desi Arnaz, Jr. The article covered a new cop show, *The Mod Squad*, starring handsome Michael Cole, and Bobby, who'd be co-starring in something called *Here Come the Brides* on ABC.

By this time, the producers at Screen Gems, which produced *Brides,* knew the power of *Tiger Beat's* audience. Without fail, we were invited to preview screenings of all of their upcoming shows. When we saw the pilot of *Here Come the Brides,* it was easy for us to spot Bobby Sherman's potential as a superstar.

We were right. From its first Wednesday night episode in September 1968, *Brides* was a hit. Bobby played Jeremy Bolt, the youngest of three brothers in 1880s Seattle. Jeremy was sweet and shy and spoke with a stammer. Bobby became an overnight *Tiger Beat* fave. We had his cute, dimpled face on the cover by the November issue.

I wasted no time making arrangements to visit the *Here Come the Brides* set at Columbia Ranch. The indoor sets of the 1880s logging town were located there, as was the forested landscape of Seattle. Hundreds of acres wide and surrounded by tall, ivy-covered fences so no one could see in, the Ranch was situated just a few blocks from the NBC Studios in Burbank. I'd been there many times, but my first visit to the *Brides* set was quite an adventure. The guard at the studio entrance gave me a map to find the set. I needed it!

I drove past soundstages and people dressed in all sorts of costumes, then past a city park with a big round fountain that would later be immortalized in the opening credits of *Friends.* Beyond that, I drove onto a suburban street where Samantha and Darrin's house from *Bewitched* and the home of Major

Nelson from *I Dream of Jeannie* sat practically side by side. I was a little sad as I passed by the jungle set where I'd watched several *Monkees* episodes shot only the year before, then onto the sets for "San Juan, Puerto Rico" and the "Convento San Tanco," as well as the A Go Go club—all from *The Flying Nun*.

I'd never met any of the stars of this new show, and I was feeling a little anxious. Before long, I spotted the captain's ship and then the whole town of 1880s Seattle, just as it looked in the pilot.

The unit publicist for the show met me, and as each of the actors took a break from filming, I was introduced to them one by one. I met Robert Brown first, and instead of shaking my hand, he grabbed it gently and kissed my fingers in a most gentlemanly way. Next I met David Soul, who was soft-spoken and oh so handsome. Robert played the oldest of the Bolt brothers, and David, the middle brother. Then I met Joan Blondell and Bridget Hanley, two lovely ladies, both as sweet as could be. Bridget, who played one of the "brides" and became Bobby's character's love interest, invited me to her dressing room, which helped put me at ease. On her dressing table, I spotted an adorable photograph of Bridget with her cheeks puffed out, chomping on an apple. "I keep this picture here," she told me, "to remind me of what I will look like if I eat too much." Before long, Bridget was called back to the set to film her next scene.

During the next break, I finally got to meet Bobby. My heart pounded as I gazed into his startling, crystal blue eyes. He leaned over and gave me a welcoming kiss on the cheek, along with his signature greeting, “Hi, babe!” At that moment, I couldn’t know how genuine Bobby’s friendliness was, or that we would become good friends, learn to trust each other, and would really enjoy working together for the next two years.

There was no doubt that Bobby was going to be *Tiger Beat*’s next superstar, and that I’d soon be working overtime coming up with stories about him. He and I decided to do our interviews during the crew’s two-hour lunch breaks, rather than squeezing in a few minutes here and there, between scenes. After a time, these interviews became routine, but they were always a pleasure. That first lunchtime interview was extra special, though, thanks to both Bobby—who drove me there in his midnight blue Rolls Royce—and the meal we shared.

When I was growing up, my mom made a really great pot roast, but we normally didn’t eat expensive cuts of meat. Bobby took me to the nearby Yankee Peddler restaurant in Burbank, where I quickly fell in love with prime rib and horseradish sauce. We both ordered a dinner meal and ate slowly as we talked. This became our routine: the Yankee Peddler, prime rib, and hours of tape-recorded interviews that I crafted into stories like the seven-part series “The Bobby Sherman Story, Told in His Own Words.”

People always want to know if I had crushes on the faves I covered for *Tiger Beat.* The truth is that these guys usually either became my friends, as Bobby did, or they were just nice people I worked with and saw once a week or more. Bobby was four years older than I and more mature, and while I was always excited to be near him, I admired him more as one would a drop-dead-gorgeous older brother than as a superstar. Bobby was friendly and easy to be around, and always made me feel comfortable. He also made my job easier by often being candid with me.

Sometimes his stories were poignant. When he was four years old, he told me, he was smaller than the other kids in his neighborhood, who shunned him. So, he invented an invisible friend. "Frank" and Bobby did everything together: They argued (Bobby always won), played games, and walked together to the candy store. Bobby and Frank stayed best friends until kindergarten, where Bobby made friends with other kids. This was exactly the kind of innocent, easy story that *TB* readers wanted to hear.

Because he happened not to be sleazy or angry about "not being taken seriously," as were some of the teen idols we dealt with, Bobby was the perfect *Tiger Beat* subject. The drama in his life involved things we could easily report, like the time he had almost set his parents' house on fire as a boy. His hobbies included clean-cut stuff like the miniature replica of Disneyland's Main Street he'd built when he was twelve and still shows off to this day. He'd been around show business—he was a protégé of Sal Mineo and "discovered" by Natalie Wood—long enough to know the ropes. He understood the importance of publicity, and was the most cooperative superstar I ever worked with.

Asked to come to the *Tiger Beat* photo studio, he'd stay as long as we needed him. When we ran a contest called "Bobby Sherman's Dream Girl Contest," he actually participated by working with me on the rules of the contest and reading every entry until he found the one he liked the most. *We received more than two million entries.*

In the October 1969 issue, we announced the winner: sixteen-year-old Sharon Baker of Victoria, Texas. She flew to Hollywood later that month, and we visited the set of *Brides*, where Bobby greeted Sharon with a big bear hug. Sharon's mom and I stayed behind when Bobby took Sharon to the Yankee Peddler; their only chaperone was *Tiger Beat*'s photographer Kenny Lieu. Of course we ran a story, titled "My Dream Date with Bobby Sherman by Sharon Baker." Where bylines were concerned, everyone was a reporter, even the contest winners.

In one story, I claimed Bobby was so nice, he'd give you the shirt off his back. (Hey, it wasn't journalism.) That inspired me to launch the "Win the Shirt Off Bobby's Back!" contest. We printed a shirtless photo of him—rare for *Tiger Beat*—on the cover of the January 1969 issue, and I went to the hippest men's store in Hollywood and bought five beautiful new shirts. Bobby posed in each one, and the winners, featured in the May 1970 issue, each won one of the shirts. A boy won Bobby's scarf, the only item of clothing he'd worn in that shirtless cover photo we'd run.

Despite the fact that Bobby had quickly become a major star, with Top Ten million-selling records and sold-out concerts across the country, *Brides* was canceled after its second season.

We'd been through a lot during those two years. I broke the news when Bobby's dog, Dopey, died after being hit by a car. I wrote about his beautiful new home in Encino. But I didn't write about his romance with and eventual marriage to Patti Carnel. Bobby knew that the wives of two of the Monkees, Samantha Dolenz and Linda Jones, had received hate mail from angry fans after their weddings. Bobby not only didn't want that to happen to Patti, he didn't want his marriage to hurt his career. So, when I did a spread about Bobby's new house, I didn't mention that Patti lived there, too. I also didn't report on how the huge four-poster bed had several film cameras pointed at it from different corners of the ceiling. In the twenty-first century, that would likely have led to a private sex tape gone viral. In 1970, *Tiger Beat* looked the other way.

Readers still demanded anything and everything about Bobby, who continued to do live concerts and appear on variety shows. We breathlessly covered his next television gig, a new series called *Getting Together* that debuted in September of 1971. In this spinoff of *The Partridge Family*, Bobby played

Bobby Conway, a songwriter in need of a lyricist. In December, I put together a special issue magazine called *Getting Together with Bobby*, which no doubt would have become a monthly or quarterly magazine if the show had lasted. But, up against the breakout CBS hit *All in the Family* on Saturday nights, *Getting Together* never caught on and was cancelled after only fourteen episodes.

I continued to work with Bobby until I left *Tiger Beat* and was honored to be among the special guests when the Variety Club of Southern California honored him with its humanitarian award "for his unexcelled work with people of all ages, and his unique ability to bridge the generation gap." It was true—pretty much everyone, even people who sneered at teen idols, was charmed by Bobby. Even when he was the biggest teen idol in America, he never failed to be the sincere, sweet person I had met that first day on the *Brides* set.

Chapter 17

The Rain, the Partridges, and Other Things

The Cowsills exploded onto the music scene in November 1967 when their hit "The Rain, the Park and Other Things" soared to number two on the Billboard pop singles chart. They went from being a garage band that played college parties to being arena headliners who appeared on every national TV show from *Ed Sullivan* to *The Tonight Show*.

The Cowsills were perfect for our teen magazine audience: wholesome young men singing pop-rock harmonies with their kid sister, eight-year-old Susan, *and their mom*. Barbara Cowsill, known to fans as Mini Mom because she was so short, didn't want to join her kids' rock band. She suffered from terrible stage fright and didn't consider herself a singer. But her husband, who controlled the Cowsills as an act and as a family, strong-armed her into pop stardom.

I met the Cowsills on their first press trip to Hollywood shortly after their first hit. They were a pleasant group and fun to be around; I remember the guys teased one another a lot, just as any group of close siblings might. We put Bill, Bob, Barry, and John Cowsill on the January 1968 cover of *Tiger Beat* and ran features and pin-ups of them for more than a year. But even though they continued to have big hits—"We Can Fly" and "Indian Lake" in 1968, and their biggest hit, "Hair," in 1969—they somehow never caught on with our readers. Fans never wrote in about being "in love" with the Cowsill boys, as they did with the Monkees, Paul Revere and the Raiders, and Dino, Desi & Billy. Even Sajid Khan, the actor from India who appeared in the 1966 movie *Maya* and the *Maya* TV series, was more popular with readers than the Cowsills. Chuck Laufer liked to brag that he knew what made a teen idol successful, but the truth is, you just never knew who was going to click with teenaged girls and who wasn't.

Today, the Cowsills are probably best remembered as the inspiration for *The Partridge Family*. Created for Screen Gems television by producers Bernard Slade and Bob Claver, the idea had originated as a sitcom featuring the Cowsills, a teen band who performed with their mom and baby sister. But Slade and Claver, after spending some time with the family, found little acting talent among the Cowsill kids. When Bud Cowsill heard that screen star Shirley Jones had been cast to play Mini Mom, he went nuts. Slade and Claver abandoned their Cowsills idea, and they commissioned a script for a show about a musical family featuring a mom, played by Shirley, who sang background. Her stepson, David Cassidy, was cast as her eldest son.

The Partridge Family debuted in September 1970, and David became an overnight sensation. Chuck had already locked up *Partridge* merchandizing and exclusive publishing rights, just as he had with *The Monkees*. He was on autopilot, securing deals for *Tiger Beat's Official Partridge Family* magazine and exclusive, open-access arrangements that would allow me and our photographers to visit the *Partridge* set as often as possible.

I'd been to the Columbia Ranch many times to watch outdoor scenes shot for both *The Monkees* and *Here Come the Brides*, but I was a little nervous the first time I drove over to the set of *The Partridge Family*. But I wasn't nervous about meeting cute David Cassidy. I was nervous about meeting Shirley Jones.

I had seen Shirley in *The Music Man* movie musical so many times. I'd played the soundtrack album in my room endlessly, all through high school; I knew every song by heart. I had danced around my room to that album, mastering a majorette air baton routine to "Seventy-Six Trombones" that pains me to think about today.

Once again, I drove past the *Bewitched* house, just up the street from the Partridges' home—which turned out to be Gladys Kravitz's house, also from *Bewitched*. Parked out front was the now-famous Partridge Family bus, painted in the style of the Dutch artist Mondrian.

I met the entire cast that first day: Shirley Jones, David Cassidy, Susan Dey, Danny Bonaduce, Suzanne Crough, and Jeremy Gelbwaks. Someone had explained to them how important *Tiger Beat* was to Screen Gems, and they all seemed as delighted to meet me as I was to meet them. When I finally got Shirley alone, I quietly told her what a huge fan I was of her work in the movie musicals *Oklahoma!* and *The Music Man*. She was so gracious, thanking me for my compliments.

But *Tiger Beat* readers were less interested in Shirley than I was. On their behalf, I was there to get to know David and Susan. Especially David.

The whole experience of covering David and the *Partridge* show was different for me. For one thing, I was twenty-three years old and no longer a peer of the people I was covering. Here, everyone except Shirley was younger than I. Also, my role at the magazine had grown. I was more responsible for all aspects of its production and sales. On this project, my focus was less on camaraderie with the stars than on gathering as much information and getting as many scoops as I could—still our advantage over New York-based *16*.

Once we began producing *Tiger Beat's Official Partridge Family* magazine, Chuck named one of my editorial assistants, Sharon Lee, as editor of that publication. She and I traveled many times to the exterior and interior *Partridge* sets, where we spent hours observing, doing interviews between takes, and gathering baby pictures (still a favorite with our readers). Because Sharon needed a ton of material for her *Partridge* magazine, she interacted more frequently with the other stars of the show. My focus was on David, who was our number one fave of 1970—and for the next several years, besides.

While *Tiger Beat* ran a monthly column about the Partridges by Danny Bonaduce's sister, Cecilia, most of the Partridge coverage in *TB* went to David. At first, David was eager and willing to use down time from shooting to talk with me and to come to our office for formal portrait shoots. But it wasn't long before he developed an attitude, and he often acted put out when Sharon and I tried to sit down for an interview. We needed a lot of material to keep up with reader demands, and David was a downright punk about it. When he spotted me hanging out on the set, and the director called "Cut, take fifteen!" he'd make a dash for his dressing room or some other hideout. He became really good at avoiding me.

When I complained about this to Chuck Laufer, he knew exactly how to handle it: the Hollywood way. He called up David's father and Shirley Jones' husband, actor Jack Cassidy, and asked Jack to have a heart-to-heart talk with David about the importance of good publicity. Chuck sweetened the deal with motorbikes for Jack and Shirley's two sons, Shaun and Patrick.

It worked. From that point on, David was reluctantly cooperative with me. This was the first time I'd encountered resistance from a teen idol. I realize now that, unlike the Monkees or Bobby Sherman, David Cassidy was younger when he became famous. His fame came almost literally overnight, and he didn't have the support system of family or peers to help him navigate this scary new life. He was on his own, facing demands on his time and his personal life, something he struggled to deal with throughout his career. I was surprised when, years later, Sharon Lee confided to me that David, forced to cooperate with *Tiger Beat* and all the other fan mags, was bitter that others were making money off of his celebrity. Who can blame him?

Susan Dey, on the other hand, was never anything but pleasant and eager to please. Just seventeen when she was cast as Laurie Partridge, she had to have a chaperone live with her in Hollywood that first year. She'd been a successful model in New York but had never acted before. She looked great on TV, but in person, I'd never seen anyone so thin. Years later, she revealed that she had been anorexic as a young girl. Few people had heard of the disease back then. We published a lot of stories about how Susan kept her perfect figure.

During an interview on the set one day, David told me how his roommate Sam's dog, Sheesh, had had a litter of five puppies. David was worried about what to do with all those puppies. He worked twelve-hour days, and it wasn't like he could put a classified ad in the newspaper: "David Cassidy's puppies, free to a good home."

"I think I can help," I told David. "What if my mom took care of the puppies at her home, and we'll run a contest in *Tiger Beat* for five of our readers to win one of your puppies?"

He loved the idea, but he wanted me to assure him he could visit the puppies during the two months it would take us to publish the contest, choose the winners, and ship the puppies to their new families. It was a one-hour drive to my mom's house in Anaheim. David really loved those puppies, and it wasn't easy for him to part with them.

I decided the puppies would go to the readers who came up with the best names for them. We received thousands of entries, and David quickly dispensed with those he didn't like. The puppies, whom David visited twice, were eventually christened Cassy (short for Cassidy), Dainty, Happy, Tiger (as in *Tiger Beat*), and Pepper, who was all black. I'd become very attached to these puppies myself, and I cried all the way from LAX to my office when the time came to ship them off to their new owners.

At first, as David's fame grew, he shared pretty much equal coverage with Bobby Sherman. Pretty soon, as Bobby's record sales declined and his new series was cancelled, his spot was taken by Donny Osmond. In the meantime, our coverage of David Cassidy followed the usual *Tiger Beat* formula: Within a month of the *Partridge* debut, we published "My Life Story by David Cassidy," a seven-part series with accompanying baby pictures. By November of 1970, we'd licensed a column called "David and Susan Tell It Like It Is," where they answered questions sent by fans. Each column began with a handwritten note from David or Susan that gave the column a little more authenticity. In the December 1970 issue, David was featured in a two-page centerfold autographed pin-up.

We'd had such great response to our "Meet Bobby Sherman" contest, and I was determined to top it. Wouldn't it be the ultimate experience for one of our readers to have a walk-on role in a *Partridge* episode, meet David, and get a kiss from him? This would take our typical "Fly to Hollywood" contest into the stratosphere.

Chuck loved the idea and made arrangements with the *PF* producers for a contest-winner walk-on. We even promoted the contest in a new way, with a special flap glued onto the cover of the March 1971 issue, announcing, "Be a TV Star, Fly to Hollywood, Win an Acting Part on *The Partridge Family*, Meet and Kiss David!" The inside front cover was a color photo of David pointing into the camera and captioned "You Can Be on TV with Me!"

We called the contest "*Tiger Beat's Partridge Family* Smile Contest," and asked each entrant to send a snapshot of herself smiling. "Remember, this is not a beauty contest," we assured readers. "The judges don't even care if you're wearing braces. It's the sincerity of the smile that counts." We also asked for twenty-five words or less on "Why *The Partridge Family* makes me smile."

While we were all busy looking at photographs of smiling teenaged girls, David was preparing for his first live concert appearance, scheduled for Seattle on March 26, 1971. He rehearsed for two and a half months with a band, a musical director, and a choreographer. I was one of the guests invited to his dress rehearsal the week before his debut.

David rehearsed in one of his two stage costumes: a red, short-sleeved tee shirt and denim overalls with an American flag embroidered on the bib. One of the suspenders was undone and hung halfway down his back. The other costume was based on one of Elvis' jumpsuits—tight white pants and a white tunic top, with white fringe hanging from each sleeve. A fringed cutout showed off his smooth chest.

Between 1965 and 1971, I'd seen some amazing concerts: the Stones, the Beatles, the Dave Clark Five, the Bee Gees, the Beach Boys, the Standells, the Who, the Mamas and the Papas, Jimi Hendrix, Cream, and James Brown among them. Maybe my expectations were high. But by now, David had scored three Top Ten hits on Billboard and knew his way around a pop song. I just didn't expect such an awkward debut.

While he could play guitar and had a good singing voice, what David didn't yet have was any dance training or stage performance skills. He had only worked as an actor up to this point, so although he'd trained with a choreographer for his stage show, his movements were clumsy and graceless. As a result, his concerts offered the same stuff I had seen at his rehearsal, which involved wiggling his bottom and pointing to someone in the audience, so that each of the 10,000 fans felt he was singing just to them. The most important part for his mostly preteen audience, his promoters knew, was seeing an idol "up close and personal" (even if it was from the nose-bleed seats).

That was how the magic happened. It was all about an almost-shirtless David Cassidy and not about putting on a "real" rock show.

After David's concert dress rehearsal, the twenty or so of us in the audience sort of gathered around him, applauding and telling him what a great job he had done. We were insincere. I realized as I drove back to the office that it didn't matter if David could sing or dance or had any stage presence. He was destined to be a huge hit with all his fans, about to make every teenybopper heart go pitter-pat. And, to be honest, that was exactly what we wanted from David. His success meant more teenyboppers buying more *Tiger Beat* magazines, more dollar-and-a-quarter booklets, more fan club sets and love bead kits. It all came down to business.

After David returned from his first concert appearances, Laudy, Sharon, and I threw a surprise birthday party for him. He was genuinely surprised and eagerly opened each and every present: hand-painted portraits, a carved soap partridge, many homemade scrapbooks, hand-crocheted afghans, a stuffed fabric guitar, and lots of poems written by fans. I gave him a case of dry roasted cashews (his favorite snack), Laudy a case of 7-Up (his favorite drink), and Sharon an original Jimi Hendrix poster. David, his sulking period now ancient history, seemed genuinely appreciative of all the attention. We wrapped up the party with a present from the entire Laufer Company of magazines: a sixteen-by-twenty-inch framed color portrait of David on stage, shot by Kenny Lieu. David was overwhelmed, and we all had a blast—not to mention a fabulous photo spread for our family of magazines. By now, David had learned how to turn on the charm.

In November of 1971, we ran the big story about our Smile Contest winner, sixteen-year-old Karen Lee Boman of Indianapolis, Indiana. On her first afternoon in town, she came to the *Tiger Beat* offices and met the Osmonds, who were there for a photo shoot. She met Bobby Sherman and watched him film an episode of *Getting Together*, and she lunched with Susan Dey and her handsome brother, Tommy. On their way out of the Yankee Peddler restaurant, she met Wes Stern, Bobby's new TV co-star. The next day, Karen had lunch with all the kids from *The Brady Bunch*.

She spent a total of two days on *The Partridge Family* set. Shirley Jones gave her words of encouragement for her upcoming role, and David's good friend, Al Rhodes, invited her to spend the day at Disneyland after she finished filming. She worked with producer Bob Claver, who helped her learn her line and gave her acting directions for the big moment.

David was incredibly kind. He spent many hours with Karen, trying to help calm her nervousness by talking about anything other than her acting debut. He signed many souvenirs, including her copy of the script and photos we had provided, for her to take home as special mementos.

For a giddy sixteen-year-old, Karen was amazingly composed and focused on her one line. She played the role of a Partridge Family fan at a record store signing party. She walked up to David and said, “Oh, Keith, you’re so wonderful,” as he autographed an album for her. (Unfortunately, that line was cut from the episode before it aired.) She said “Thank you” as he handed her the album and a hamster in a little cage, then she walked off the set past Shirley Jones and Dave Madden.

After three takes, the scene was perfect. Karen was rewarded with a kiss from David, just as our contest had promised, as well as enough teen idol memories to last a lifetime. My only regret is that we never followed up with Karen, as we’d done with the winners of the puppy contest.

When I think back about my years with *Tiger Beat*, these are the experiences I treasure most. It was interesting, being so close to the stars, but I was more interested in bringing fans closer to their idols. When we arranged for readers to have these amazing experiences, I was proud to be a small part of their happiness.

Chapter 18

Getting Groovy with the Osmonds

I wasn't yet editor of *Tiger Beat* when I first saw the Osmonds. I was just an eleven-year-old girl who was lucky enough to grow up two miles from Disneyland, which meant I got to go to Disneyland often—and the Osmonds, before they were world-famous, worked there.

My brother and I always got Disneyland ticket books in our Christmas stockings, and because it was such a safe place, we went there without our parents. Usually we'd go with friends—Disneyland was our own personal playground. Unlike the tourists who had to cram in as many rides as they could because they were visiting from far away, we'd sometimes go on only a few rides, spending more of our time on Tom Sawyer's Island, having caricature portraits drawn by Walt Disney's brother Roy (who drew all day in front of Sleeping Beauty's Castle) and enjoying the "extra" attractions of Disneyland like the Dapper Dans, the barbershop quartet who sang on Main Street most days. It was during one of these many visits that I first saw the Osmonds.

As I later reported in *Tiger Beat*, the Osmonds wound up with their Disneyland gig in 1958, during a trip to Hollywood from their home in Utah. They were in town auditioning for a guest spot on *The Lawrence Welk Show*, and after being turned down by the casting director, their parents drove the four boys, Alan, 9; Wayne, 7; Merrill, 5; and Jay, 3, over to Disneyland for a little fun. The story goes that they were still dressed in matching pants, shirts, and vests when they met the Dapper Dans on Main Street. The Dans asked if the boys could sing along, and the Dans' lead singer was so impressed with the four youngsters, he introduced them to Walt Disney.

By the summer of 1960, the Osmond Brothers were making summer appearances at Disneyland, strolling along Main Street as a pint-sized barbershop quartet. In 1962, they moved their act to the Plaza Gardens and then on to the Golden Horseshoe as an opening act for the Golden Horseshoe Review. Over the years, I saw and enjoyed them a number of times at Disneyland. But by the time they became regulars on *The Andy Williams Show* in 1962—a regular role that lasted until early 1970—I was a sophomore in high school and had moved on to other artists.

But millions of other girls were tuning in to *Andy Williams* to see Alan, Wayne, Merrill, Jay, and little Donny, who'd been added to the act. The group hadn't had their first hit record yet, but the bags of mail we received about them at *Tiger Beat* proved they had a fan following that wanted "pix 'n' fax" on the boys. We obliged: "Bring on the Osmond Brothers" was our introduction of this super group in the October 1968 issue.

The whole family (except older brothers Tom and Virl) had moved to Hollywood by this time, and I was invited to interview them at their rented home in Westwood, next to Beverly Hills. It was not a fancy star mansion, just a house big enough for the whole family, chosen because of its proximity to the Mormon Temple on Santa Monica Boulevard.

From the very first moment, the Osmonds were friendly and really impressed me as a normal, all-American family—except that they all possessed exceptional talents. I never heard my parents quarrel or shout, and I got that same feeling with this family: They all seemed to genuinely love one another. The Osmond parents, Olive and George, were the sweetest couple.

As usual, our first story offered detailed profiles of each of the five Osmonds, although I'm sorry to report that we misspelled Donny's name as "Donnie" in that and the next several articles. By that time, we'd shifted our focus to bigger fave-raves Bobby Sherman, Davy Jones, Sajid Khan, and Jack Wild. The Osmonds appeared to have run their short, sweet course as potential teen idols.

In early 1970, the group reimagined itself as a pop act, trading in its squeaky-clean, crew-cut image for longer hair and choreographed dance routines. In the March 1970 issue, we ran a full color photo of the newly groovy Osmonds and mentioned in the accompanying article that they had a new record coming out soon.

The mail we received made it apparent that Donny was the favorite of the group. When I was in Las Vegas, I had a chance to see why. There to see the opening of Elvis' latest show at The International Hotel, I received an invitation from Frank Sinatra to be a guest at his daughter Nancy's new nightclub act. The Osmonds were also on the bill.

I'm sure the Chairman of the Board wasn't thrilled that I didn't love Nancy's show, which I reviewed for *NME*. I wrote, "Though it was evident that she tried very hard to put together a well-rounded Vegas act, her show was more a parody of a Las Vegas stage show. Eleven male dancers joined Nancy on her opening number and waltzed her round the stage. Her first four numbers were all ballads, so slow the audience hardly knew the star had made her way onto the stage, for they continued to talk loudly over drinks."

I did, however, like the Osmonds. A lot. "Bounding on stage, they opened their portion of the show with a Motown medley," I wrote. "A super-stirring 'He Ain't Heavy, He's My Brother' not only brought the house to life, but primed them for the real knockout number in the show, 'That's Life,' sung by the Osmonds' youngest brother, six-year-old Jimmy!"

That night, I became a true Osmond fan. They were accomplished musicians and dancers—boy, could they move!—and their vocal harmonies were rich and well-arranged.

I was in the front row for the celebrity-packed opening night performance (which Elvis also attended), and returned the next day to photograph the Osmonds hanging out in their hotel room and later in their dressing room at Caesars. At that second show, I got some fabulous on-stage shots, all of which were featured in a four-page *Tiger Beat* spread titled "Day and Night with the Osmonds." They had dropped "brothers" from the name of the group.

We typically stayed away from religion when writing about faves, but their Mormon faith was so important to the Osmonds, we decided to tackle that fact head-on in the pages of *Tiger Beat*. One of our earliest articles about the group was a somewhat out-of-character piece titled "The Osmonds: How God Fills Our Lives." They were always very open about their dedication to their religion, and unlike a lot of show business people, they didn't just talk the talk, they walked the walk.

The Osmonds were among the most dedicated performers I knew. In September of that year, Donny was hospitalized with a 105-degree temperature. I had spent that Saturday afternoon with the family while they taped *American Bandstand*, and Donny seemed fine. After four hours of *Bandstand* taping, the guys headed across town to CBS studios to rehearse *The Glen Campbell Goodtime Hour*. After wrapping up that rehearsal, Donny began to feel bad, and Mrs. Osmond took him straight to the hospital, where the next day I got an exclusive shot of Donny in his hospital bed, reading a fan letter with an IV stuck in his arm. It turned out to be a bad case of the 24-hour flu, and Donny was back singing with his brothers by the time *Glen*

Campbell taped a few nights later.

In 1971, the Osmonds had their first break-out hit, "One Bad Apple," which went to number one on the Billboard charts. All this was happening while David Cassidy was hugely popular, and I was buried in Partridge-mania. When the Osmonds invited me along to shoot a commercial for a Japanese soft drink in the mountains of Colorado, I sent my editorial assistant, Sharon Lee, in my place. Sharon had the time of her life, and her photos of the Osmonds—on their private plane and filming their commercial in ankle-deep snow, wearing matching ski sweaters and hats—made a wonderful *Tiger Beat* spread we called "The Osmonds' Winter Wonderland."

By June of that year, Donny and/or the Osmonds were on just about every *Tiger Beat* cover. Mrs. Osmond was always gracious about my many interview and photo shoot requests. I've read in recent years that she was upset with the way *16* portrayed Donny, and she hated that Gloria Stavers ran shirtless photos of her young son. If that's true, it might be why the Osmonds were always so cooperative and generous with me and *Tiger Beat*. We understood that modesty was an important part of their religion, and I did my best to honor that. Anyway, Donny was just as popular fully clothed.

We introduced eleven-year-old Marie to readers in the June issue that year. At that point, she was only appearing with the Osmonds when they performed in Japan. In the next issue, we published the first installment of her exclusive column, "My

Brothers by Marie Osmond." Also in June, we announced a new contest: "Be Adopted by the Osmonds." The lucky winner would spend an entire week with the Osmonds. Contestants had to guess how many photos of the Osmonds *Tiger Beat* had published from May 1970 to May 1971. The exact number was 163, and the winner was Pam Turner from Richardson, Texas.

I was Pam's tour guide for her all-Osmonds week. One night was a special dinner out at Stefanino's in Hollywood, the next day horseback riding and a picnic in Griffith Park. I could have had the picnic catered, but instead I volunteered to make all the picnic food, including my sister-in-law's teriyaki chicken and her mother's potato salad, which was much like American potato salad, but with a bag of mixed vegetables and a can of tuna stirred in. (Don't turn up your nose until you've tried it—it's fabulous.)

In between visits with the Osmonds, I took Pam out to Columbia Ranch, where she toured the former *Here Come the Brides* set with Bobby Sherman. We also visited the *Partridge Family* set, where she met the entire cast and went to lunch with David Cassidy and his best friend, Sam Hyman. There was the requisite day at Disneyland, where the Osmonds rode every ride twice and even recalled their "old days" with a little barbershop harmony on "Side by Side." Pam also attended an Osmonds recording session, where I got a photo of her behind the microphone, singing along with Merrill and Jay.

This one did so well, I followed it up with a "Win a Lock of Donny's Hair!" contest. I tagged along to one of his haircut appointments at Little Joe's Artistic Tonsorial Parlor, photographed the trim, then scooped up some of Donny's hair. He picked the five winners at random and sent a personal note with each lock of hair. Everything we did with the Osmonds was fan-centered, and they were always eager to please.

Donny called me one day to ask for my help. I already knew about the Osmond family gift-giving tradition: When one of them celebrated a birthday, instead of the birthday boy or girl receiving gifts, he or she would give a gift to each member of the family. With their super-busy schedule, Donny explained, they had not kept up the tradition for the last two years. His fourteenth birthday was coming up on December 9, and he wanted to re-establish their family tradition. Could I help him?

Together, we planned a stealth "photo shoot" birthday party at my Hollywood apartment. About three blocks south of the *Tiger Beat* building on Highland Avenue, my new place was in a wonderful Spanish-designed building named El Cabrillo, built by Cecil B. DeMille in 1928 to house movie actors visiting from out of town. The walls were twelve-inch-thick adobe, and in my apartment, there was an entry hall alcove intended for a statue of the Virgin Mary. The living room had twelve-foot ceilings with transom windows and decorative wrought iron stair railings.

I took Donny shopping for the gifts he planned to hand out, telling his parents we were doing a photo shoot at *Tiger Beat*. Back at my place, we wrapped all the presents with my own stash of special wrapping papers and ribbons.

We got the Osmonds to my apartment by telling them we wanted to photograph them in the courtyard with the beautiful Spanish-tiled fountain in the middle, and they were surprised and delighted when our ruse was revealed. After a dinner of chili and cornbread that I cooked for everyone, we settled around the fireplace to open gifts. It was like Christmas. Donny was startled when I brought out a huge present—a large, framed photo of him singing onstage taken by our photographer, Kenny Lieu—with a card that read "Happy Birthday from all your friends at the Laufer Company." For the next hour, he opened birthday gifts fans had sent to *Tiger Beat*. Kenny's photo of Donny sitting in front of my living room fireplace ran with my story, "Donny Came to My House."

In that article, I wrote about how Donny had come up to me after all the presents were opened and stammered an apology for not having anything for me. His voice trailed off, and he blushed. Then he leaned over and spoke softly into my ear. "But I know what I'm going to get for you." I wanted to tell him I didn't want anything, that this night was all the thanks I needed, but I was so surprised, I didn't say anything.

A few days later, a heavy package arrived for me with no return address. Inside was a beautiful set of hammered copper cooking pans that gleamed like soft gold. Enclosed was a note: "To the best cooker of birthday dinners in the world, from the boy who had the best birthday in the world! (I told you I knew what I was going to get you). Love, Donny."

I used that beautiful cookware constantly as I tried to improve my cooking skills, and I purchased a wrought iron hanger to dangle the pots above the stove, where I would see them every day and be reminded of our special connection.

Early in 1972, I was invited to brother Tommy Osmond's wedding reception. Only Mormons who are over eighteen and have a "temple recommend" may attend the actual marriage ceremony in the Temple. George and Olive gave me permission to take pictures at the reception, and I got some beautiful shots of the bridesmaids in lovely floor-length gowns and the Osmond guys in tuxedos with white ruffled shirts piped in red—*very* early 1970s.

Donny, Jay, and I decorated the couple's car, attaching balloons and shaving cream and covering the car with lipstick messages. Donny filled the whole car with letters from fans, while Jay filled the hubcaps with rocks and tied soda cans to the back bumper. I helped some, but I was also madly shooting pictures of this amazing scene. A great photo of Donny and Jay in their wild tuxes filled the cover of the April 1972 *Tiger Beat*.

The next morning, I joined Alan and Donny for breakfast. When I ordered my usual morning cup of tea, I got a lecture from Donny. "You shouldn't drink tea," he advised. "It has caffeine, and that's bad for you." He didn't press the issue, but it was the nearest thing to criticism I ever heard from anyone in the Osmond clan. They tended to quietly follow their beliefs.

That afternoon, I drove up to the Osmonds' ranch just outside Ogden and shot pictures for a photo spread. Back in Hollywood, I asked each of the guys to write captions for the photos I had taken—a nice spread in *Tiger Beat* and yet another Osmonds exclusive.

Some years later, Sharon Lee, who had taken my place as editor when I left *Tiger Beat*, called and asked me to write an update on the Osmonds for the magazine's fifteenth anniversary issue. I was living in Utah at the time, so it was easy for me to drive to Provo, where most of the family was living, and do an interview. I spent a lovely afternoon catching up with Merrill Osmond, who filled me in on what each of the Osmonds was doing in 1979. The Osmonds had built their own TV studio in Provo where they filmed *The Donny and Marie Show* in the late 1970s. I remember feeling grateful that my association with the Osmonds had blossomed into a lasting friendship with this very "real" family.

Chapter 19

Elvis Goes to Vegas (and I Follow)

The day of Elvis' July 1969 concert in Las Vegas finally arrived. I left early in the morning, hoping to avoid much of the desert summer sun, because my VW Bug had no air conditioning. By noon, it was 107 degrees in my tiny car, even with both windows rolled down. The air-conditioned lobby of the brand-new International Hotel, with its ten-foot-high letters spelling out Elvis' name, felt wonderful.

The Colonel had arranged for a carnival-themed Elvis fantasyland, with young women in straw hats handing out free Elvis swag. Comical and exciting at the same time, there were custom-made banners, pennants, posters, oversized cardboard records, and Elvis pictures plastered on every pillar and wall, both inside and outside the hotel. Nick Naff, the International's publicity director, gave me a tour of the thirty-story hotel. It had been open less than a month and, with 1,500 rooms, was the biggest hotel in the world. The main showroom seated 2,000 and was the largest room of its kind anywhere, with a sixty-foot-wide stage bigger than Radio City Music Hall's in New York City. The International set out to capture a first-class clientele with

Japanese, Italian, French, and Bavarian restaurants and crystal chandeliers imported from Czechoslovakia. Each floor was decorated in Spanish, French provincial, and Oriental decor—as far removed as could be from the Vegas strip hotels with their five-cent slot machines and two-dollar buffets.

After my tour (during which I'd peeked into the lounge showroom where Ike and Tina Turner were rehearsing), I killed an hour on the quarter slots and watched tourists play roulette, craps, and blackjack until the showroom opened. My mom had made me a sleeveless, embroidered lace mini-dress from the latest French *Vogue* pattern book. It was simple but elegant, and I felt stunning.

Unlike the concerts presented in Vegas today, the Elvis shows back then followed the traditions of an old-time Vegas dinner show. When the magic hour arrived, I was led to a table just to the right of center stage—as front-row-center as I could get. From my seat, after dinner, I could see Elvis arrive in the wings.

"Elvis live, again!" I wrote in my *NME* article. "And I was there to see it for you!" I went on to promise that Elvis could hold his own with the new stars of the day, and pointed out that even the deep breaths he drew between songs elicited applause. He performed medleys of all his hits, as well as new material like "Memories," which he'd introduced on the comeback special. Designed by Bill Belew, Elvis' black tunic shirt with the four-inch turned-up collar would very soon be copied by everyone from the Osmonds to the Jackson 5, but on that night, it was an original.

So, too, was his humble approach to his audience. "I'd like to do my latest release; it's been a big seller for me," he told us, then added shyly, "something I really needed." He performed two Beatles songs and introduced a new song, "Suspicious Minds," which would go on to be another million-seller for him. He wrapped things up with the Ray Charles hit "What'd I Say," clutching the microphone, shaking his legs, and doing karate punches as he screamed the lyrics. Almost before the song ended, Elvis walked off the stage to a standing ovation.

As Elvis performed his encore number, "I Can't Help Falling in Love," Graylon slipped behind me and whispered in my ear, "There's a press conference in Room C3. Get there as fast as you can!"

I practically ran to the conference room, where I grabbed a chair in the front row. Elvis greeted us by saying, "I'm really beat. That was the fourth time I did that show today," referring to the three dress rehearsals he'd done earlier in the day. He didn't look beat; he looked confident as he basked in the glow of a wonderful performance. He answered questions for more than an hour, after which Col. Parker told us if we'd like to have a picture taken with Elvis, to please line up. I was third in line for that opportunity, and I have the greatest picture of me looking up into his handsome face. He shook my hand, and, when I told him how much I'd enjoyed his show, he replied with his trademark, “Thank you very much.”

I raced back to my hotel room, typed out my story about the show for *NME*, and the next morning, took a cab to the nearest post office so I could send my copy out via airmail, the fastest way to get written material overseas at the time. Back at the hotel, I worked up the courage to ask Nick Naff if I might take pictures of that night’s performance. Absolutely no cameras were allowed at Elvis’ shows, and I don’t know why Nick gave me the okay. “You can shoot the late show from the balcony, but absolutely no flash!”

I agreed. I had my 35mm portraiture telephoto lens, but there was no way it could do the job of shooting Elvis on stage from the balcony. I called around to the Vegas photography stores and managed to rent a 250mm telephoto lens for my Nikon. I bought rolls of 400 ASA film—the highest speed film available—and passed the remaining hours at Ike and Tina Turner’s early show in the lounge. Tina was a powerhouse performer, but all I could think about was shooting that night’s 11 p.m. Elvis performance.

When the time came, I was escorted up to the balcony. I felt like I’d been given a very special gift, and also like I was on a mission for the CIA—everything was so secretive! I shot sixty-four slides that night, returned the lens to the camera store the next morning, and headed back to LA. I took the film to the best photo-processing lab in town, knowing that shooting from such a distance, even with fast film, didn’t ensure that the images would come out. The manager promised they'd "push" the film—meaning they'd develop it for a longer period of time—so the images would be more likely to come through.

I was still nervous when I picked up the slides three days later. I needn't have worried: Every single color shot turned out fantastic. I published a few of these pictures in *Tiger Beat,* and a few in *NME,* all of them in black and white. *NME* didn't print color, and in *Tiger Beat* the color pages were reserved for the most popular faves. Although Elvis had reclaimed his status as the King of Rock 'n' Roll in the rest of the world, in *Tiger Beat* he was "just" another legend.

Seven months later, I was back in Vegas for a second round of Elvis engagements at the International. "I just can't keep away," I admitted in my *NME* piece. "Elvis is a habit-forming 'drug' that does you good!" Although he had the flu when I saw him this time, the act was even better than it had been before.

As I prepared my latest set of Elvis stories, I had no idea that my next contact with the King would be as a part of his next movie.

"I wasn't a bikini-clad teenager dancing the Watusi to a lame Elvis musical number," I always say when I mention I was in an Elvis movie. "And I wasn't an extra in the stands as he sped around a racetrack." Instead, I was in the Elvis movie most people have never heard of.

I was in *Elvis: That's the Way It Is,* a 1970 documentary directed by filmmaker Denis Sanders. The movie documents

Elvis' Vegas shows of the summer before and showcases his return to live performances. Most of the concert footage in the original film was shot at the International, intercut with scenes of Elvis and his band rehearsing and from the Elvis Appreciation Society convention in Luxembourg.

The original cut of the movie, released in 1970, also included interviews with an assortment of fans, interspersed throughout the film. "You don't have an entertainer without an audience," Denis told me. "The effect on Elvis' audience is as much a part of the drama as the entertainer himself."

Denis told me he didn't know much about Presley fans, but knew he wanted people of different ages and cultures. "That's how I found you," he told me. "One of the Elvis fans said, 'Go see Ann Moses!'"

I was thrilled when Denis said he wanted to interview me for the film, but also nervous as could be. Although I was completely comfortable among Hollywood celebrities, I'd still get nauseated whenever I had to speak on camera or make a live appearance. I always preferred being behind the camera or on the other end of an interview.

In August of 1970, I made my way to Vegas, where Denis was shooting footage for the documentary and where Elvis was performing again. Later that month, Denis came to my *Tiger Beat* office and interviewed me on-camera. I nervously answered his questions, and then they shot footage of me walking down the hall and talking with our art editor.

The movie includes footage of me watching Elvis from my stage-side seat and the interview in my office. I talk about my responsibilities as editor of *Tiger Beat* and about what it means to be an Elvis fan.

"It's so hard to describe what an Elvis fan is," I say. "It's a phenomenon like falling in love. You can't describe how it happens; it's just you're in love and you know it, and it's the same with being an Elvis fan."

Some of the moments with the other fans are really great. There's a nerdy guy who calls Elvis "the Willie Mays of Entertainment" and tells Denis, "If I don't like your film, I'm going to write you a dirty little letter." There's the 50ish, grey-haired woman and her 80ish, white-haired mother, who says she likes Elvis "because he's a religious boy and he respects his parents." Then her daughter tells us, "Mother likes lots of action. She doesn't like it when they shoot him from the waist up. She likes to see him move, and I admit I do, too. He sets my Phi Beta Kappa key a janglin'."

When the movie was finished, Denis invited me and some of my friends to a private screening at MGM studios. He also showed us outtakes that hadn't made it into the finished film. The one I'll never forget is of Elvis bending over to kiss the women in the front row as he sang "Love Me Tender." When Elvis kissed *me*, it wasn't a quick peck, but a tender, real kiss—even if it was in front of 2,000 people. Although that shot didn't make it into the movie, the kiss—and seeing it on the big screen—is etched in my memory forever.

When *That's the Way It Is* was re-cut in 2001, my part and the footage of the other fans were both deleted in favor of additional concert footage. In August of 2014, an eight-CD, two-DVD box set was released that included the original cut of the film. Happily, I was asked to write some liner notes for this box set. It was a chance to relive the excitement of those shows, and to dwell on that kiss from Elvis, one last time.

Chapter 20

Not Everyone Was a Teen Idol

The question I'm asked more than any other about my years at *Tiger Beat* is "What was __________ really like?" Although I met hundreds of famous people through my work, I didn't always have a chance to really get to know them, even when we spent a great deal of time together over several years. Other times, I became friends with the celebrities I worked with, as I did with Bobby Sherman and the Osmonds.

Some of my strongest memories of that time involve people I met once or twice, and not always for the nicest reasons. My brief encounters with Harry Nilsson were memorable because Harry was such a great guy.

Harry and I met in 1967, when RCA Records publicity head Graylon Landon asked me to write about Harry as a favor. Harry had just signed a contract with RCA, and I was happy to help Graylon, who was a valuable contact in covering Elvis Presley for my *New Musical Express* column.

Harry had been writing songs and recording demos for some years, but solo success had eluded him. He'd kept his night job at a bank. After a brief interview with Harry, I asked him to over for dinner sometime. He eagerly accepted. He was a bachelor at the time and told me he liked a home-cooked meal.

I was nervous about preparing dinner. I made one of my mother's best recipes: the braised pork chops with apples recipe I'd made for Maurice Gibb, with rice pilaf as the side dish. I wasn't twenty-one yet, so I got a friend to buy some wine for me. I wasn't crazy about wine, so I chose a Liebfraumilch, a white German wine that is on the sweet side, which, for me, made it drinkable.

Harry loved the food, and we had a lovely evening. He probably asked me more questions than I asked him: Who was my favorite interview? What was the best concert I'd ever seen? What type of music did I listen to at home? How did I get my job at *Tiger Beat*?

I was just as curious about this obviously talented man. How did he get ideas for his songs? How did he write the music—at the piano? With a guitar?

Sometime later, Harry reciprocated by inviting me out to dinner at a little Hollywood French bistro. This meal was better than the one I'd prepared, and the camaraderie was just as superb.

Eventually, Harry's career started to take off. One of his first recordings for RCA in 1967 was a song called "Cuddly Toy" that was covered by the Monkees, which gave his career a boost. Not long after our second dinner, Harry met John Lennon, his hero, and became involved with the Beatles. After that, I no longer ran into him around RCA or at the Hollywood haunts where I'd seen him before.

I was happy to go from being a friend to being one of Harry's adoring fans. At the top of my list was his 1971 concept album, *The Point!*, commissioned as the soundtrack for an ABC television special. The songs tell the story of a boy who's different but good just the same. I loved the music and the moral, and as the parent of two bi-racial boys, I played this album for them often.

That same year, I met Kurt Russell, who'd just starred in *Follow Me, Boys!* for Disney. The publicity shots the Disney studio sent over made it clear that Kurt definitely had that *Tiger Beat* "look," and I made an appointment to interview him at the Disney studios, where he was shooting a new picture.

Although I'd worked at Disneyland and met Walt Disney, it was still thrilling to visit the Disney studios. I'd been a huge fan of the daily Mouseketeers TV show as a kid, and it was exciting to tour the lot where it was filmed, as well as the offices of the Disney animators, artists, and executives.

I met Kurt and his mom, Louise, on one of the huge Disney soundstages, and found him more eager to talk about becoming a major-league baseball player than about his acting career. I interviewed him many times over the years, and he was always very unaffected and kind. My favorite memory of Kurt was when, about three years later, photographer Kenny Lieu shot

Kurt and me riding his horses near his family home in Thousand Oaks.

Once again, I became a fan of Kurt's (I loved his movie with partner Goldie Hawn called *Overboard*), as did my boys. When they were around four or five years old, they were addicted to John Carpenter's movie *Big Trouble in Little China*, in which Kurt starred. I taped that one off the TV, and my boys watched it over and over again, loving it more each time.

Not everyone was as sweet as Kurt Russell. Michael Parks, for instance, was perhaps the meanest fave since Mike Nesmith. No. He was worse! (What is it with me and meanies named Michael?)

"My Groovy Day with Michael Parks" ran in the February 1970 *Tiger Beat*, but in truth, my day with the star of the TV series *Then Came Bronson* was anything but groovy. *Bronson* was the story of a disillusioned former newspaper reporter who sets out on his motorcycle to crisscross America, sometimes learning from those he meets, sometimes offering them his own insight.

My story went on to talk about how nice Michael was, how he loved his wife and children—the usual *Tiger Beat* blah, blah, blah. Because of course I couldn't write about how he was an arrogant, belligerent pig, and that meeting him had turned out to be the number one worst day in my seven years with *Tiger Beat*.

I had gone to a lot of effort to interview Michael. I flew alone to Phoenix, stayed all night in a hotel, got up before sunrise and rode out to the location set in the Arizona desert in a studio limo—the last cool air I would feel until sundown. I was always excited when I experienced new places and people. I had never dreamed this would turn out to be a totally shitty day.

Not only was Michael Parks not nice to me, he ignored me most of the morning. I shot a few pictures of him while the cameras were rolling, but after each shot, Michael scowled at me. Finally, the unit publicist got Michael to sit down for an interview during lunch. He answered my first few questions, then he really let me have it.

"What kind of a photographer are you?" he demanded. "A true artist would wait all day for the one perfect picture, not be shooting constantly to get as many mediocre photos as possible in one day. If you were worth anything, you'd have the patience and the eye to know when to capture the one best shot!"

It was like being berated by a critical parent or an overwrought boss. I gritted my teeth and held my tongue; I wasn't about to call him out on his nasty behavior. I was twenty-two; he was thirty-one years old—an "older man" from whom I expected some maturity. Instead, his ego was out of control, and he seemed to find pleasure in belittling me at every opportunity.

I stuck out my assignment, sneaking in a few more pictures because I knew how many we'd need for both *Tiger Beat* and *FaVe!* cover shots and future stories. Not only was I wrung out from the blinding sun and 100-plus-degree heat of the outdoor shoot, but also from the tongue-lashing I'd received from superstar Michael Parks.

I held myself together on the flight home to LA, but the minute I closed the door to my apartment, I broke down in tears that didn't stop for an hour. Thank goodness Michael Parks was never a hit with *TB* readers, and I never had to endure him ever again. *Bronson* limped through a single season and was cancelled. Michael didn't work much after that, and his career is mostly forgotten—but I've never forgotten how needlessly cruel he was to a young girl one day in 1970.

Roger Daltrey, on the other hand, was much more charming.

We first introduced the Who—Daltrey, Pete Townshend, John Entwistle and Keith Moon—to *Tiger Beat* readers in Derek Taylor's "Group Scoops" column in April 1966. The following month, I wrote about how the band liked to destroy its instruments onstage after each performance.

I first saw them perform at the Monterey Pop Festival in June of 1967, and nothing could have prepared me for the experience of seeing them live. They were the most intense group I'd ever seen, putting boundless energy into every performance.

The following summer, when the Who came back to the US, I arranged to interview them for both *NME* and *Tiger Beat*. I somehow decided it would be fun to also do a photo shoot in

Hollywood's Ferndell Park. We were all a bit overdressed for a day of frolicking outdoors: John and Keith in hip British suits, Pete in a psychedelic jacket and slacks, and Roger in a tee shirt with an embroidered vest and slacks. I was wearing a mod pinstriped pantsuit.

We called the story "The Who—Kids for a Day" and summed it up with a deck that read, "Join this laughable and lovable bunch of 'nuts' on their day as kids."

I felt like a kid, too, swinging on the swings as Roger pushed me higher and higher and going down the sliding boards with this hot new rock act. After playing in the children's playground, we took a long stroll through the fern-lined paths where episodes of *Star Trek: Deep Space Nine* would later be filmed.

A few days later, I stopped in at a record company meet-and-greet for the band, held in a fancy ballroom of the hotel where they were staying. On this night, the Who were dressed up in Edwardian-style suits straight from Carnaby Street. Roger was wearing a dark blue velvet jacket, tight-fitting dress slacks, a cream-colored silk shirt, and a cranberry silk scarf. Dreamy!

At one point in the evening, Roger and I were chatting about the day we'd spent in the park, making small talk and being polite—until he leaned in close and whispered, "Would you like to come up to my room?"

I wasn't a virgin, but I wasn't a groupie, either. Even though I knew exactly what his question meant, I whispered back, “What would we be doing up in your room?”

Roger replied, “I’m sure we can think of something.”

Instead of being open to something new and probably exciting, I gave in to my lack of sexual confidence and politely declined. Oh, if only I could have a do-over! Roger Daltrey was yummy, and I can only imagine what I might have learned while we were having “fun.”

Of course, I likely wouldn’t have ever met any of these people if I hadn’t first met Derek Taylor in 1965. Derek was a kind and generous person who turned his time as the Beatles’ publicist into an opportunity to come to America, where he supported his wife and six children by starting his own public relations firm. We first met when I did an interview with the Byrds for *Rhythm ’n’ News*.

Derek treated me like I was any other professional journalist, not some teenager working for a small circulation mimeographed “newspaper” sold in Southern California record stores. His faith in me led to that interview with Ralph Benner and my job at *Tiger Beat*.

Derek and I had a fabulous working relationship. I helped him promote some of his lesser-known groups, and he helped arrange for me to do things like go on tour with the Raiders. Our close ties got me front-and-center at the Monterey Pop Festival, the cultural high point in pop music.

There was only one weird moment between Derek and me. After some routine PR work in his office on Sunset Boulevard one day, he made a pass at me. I was shocked, but determined to be polite. I stepped back, smiled, and thanked him again for a productive day. In my head I was screaming, “Ewwwww!” because Derek was fifteen years older than I, not to mention married with six children. I’m sure the expression on my face betrayed my attempt to be cool and collected, but to his credit, he was nice about me beating a hasty retreat. We worked together for many more years, and Derek remained charming and gentlemanly ever after. This bizarre moment was neither mentioned nor repeated.

Chapter 21

Real Life Beckons: Bye-Bye, Hollyweird!

Things were pretty much "*Tiger Beat* business as usual" for me over the next couple of years. I continued to visit soundstages to interview the biggest TV stars, continued to cover David and Donny and whoever else was huge with young girls at the moment. But not long after I began dating my future husband, I began craving a "normal" life. I began to wonder how life would be without any Hollywood phonies, rock star heartbreaks, or entitled celebrities. The seemingly "normal" process of going steady, moving in together, and then marrying Don just felt right.

I look back now, wondering what I was thinking or feeling when Don and I were dating. I kept no journal then, so I can only guess that the thought of settling down seemed better to me than it turned out to be. Don and I loved going to Elvis performances together, but as a couple we really didn't relish our time alone together. We never took a vacation, although we tried once. We drove up to Lake Tahoe for a long weekend, but once we were there, we didn't fancy gambling, couldn't figure out anything else to do, and drove back home before the day was over. Something was wrong with this picture, but we weren't analyzing our life together. We were young and living day to day.

Don wasn't a bad guy. He was a good man, and he cared for me. At the same time, even before we actually tied the knot, he was jealous of my "fame." I never considered myself "famous," but it bothered him that I got attention when we went to a concert, a screening, or a movie premiere. He didn't like being "Mr. Ann Moses."

In an effort to keep peace at home, I slowly began to back off from many of the things I loved about my job at *Tiger Beat*. I no longer went on tour with *anyone*, I sent associate editors to record release parties, and I gave away concert tickets to friends and co-workers. Instead of rubbing elbows with celebrities, we had old friends come up to our Hollywood apartment for barbeque dinners, or we all went out to a great Italian restaurant a few blocks from our apartment.

Don did accompany me to Tommy Osmond's wedding in Salt Lake City—the first time either of us had been there. I found the city to be beautiful, with lots to see and discover in our free time, but Don just moped his way through the entire three days.

When I got back to work, things were happening. In January of 1972, Laufer had launched yet another new publication called *Right On!*, which featured the Jackson 5, Diana Ross, the Temptations, Stevie Wonder, and other black stars of the day. For some reason, Chuck had hired a young white woman, Judy Weider, as the editor of this magazine.

With all the new magazines, we'd outgrown our offices, and needed more room for the staffs of *Tiger Beat, FaVe!, Tiger Beat's Partridge Family Magazine, Rona Barrett's Hollywood* and *Right On!* So we relocated from 1800 North Highland Avenue to 7060 Hollywood Boulevard.

I was excited about the move and got busy trying to decide on the wall and carpet color for my new office. I didn't dream this exciting move would set in motion the events that led to my resignation from *Tiger Beat.*

When we moved, Ralph ordered a new desk, so he offered me his old one, bigger than the one I'd been using for a while and made of beautiful wood in perfect condition. As I cleared out his old desk, I found a slip of paper on which Ralph had written the salaries of each of the magazine editors then working at Laufer. I was dumbstruck by what I saw.

My salary was the highest of the editors of the teen magazines, which made sense. I'd been there for six years, longer than anyone, and running the flagship publication in our chain. But according to this note, I was earning half of what Bill Royce, the editor of the just-launched *Rona Barrett's Hollywood,* was being paid.

I grabbed my handbag, walked out of the office, and drove home, shaking. I felt betrayed by the people to whom I'd devoted my energy, creativity, and heart for so many years. I was pretty sure *Rona Barrett's Hollywood* wasn't even out of the red at that time, and its editor was making twice my salary!

I knew the sad fact, even then, that men were typically paid more than women—often far more. In early 1972, America was on the cusp of Women's Liberation and raising the standards of "equal pay for equal work." In the meantime, many of us still believed it was our duty as married women to follow our husband's lead in a relationship. Which is why I decided to do what my husband suggested, and leave *Tiger Beat*.

Once I got home, I broke down. I couldn't stop crying. It was so unfair. How could all I had given be so unappreciated? I poured out my heart to Don. We'd been married for two and a half years, and I knew he didn't like that I earned four times his own salary. He was sympathetic, but he told me that quitting my job would make a statement about equal pay for women. Looking back, I think this was a way for Don to remedy the fact that his wife earned more than he did. At the time, I was too hurt to make much sense of things. I do remember being startled by Don's immediate reaction to my news, though.

"Why don't you quit, and we'll move to Northern California?"

He suggested this because we had friends in Northern California, and because he was anxious to leave his job as a commercial artist at a tiny art studio in Hollywood, a job he didn't like and for which he wasn't paid much. For some reason, Don really wanted to work in a sporting goods store. He liked the outdoors and felt he'd make a good salesman.

The next day, I went in to work and confronted Ralph about what I'd discovered. His reaction was to offer an alibi: The reason they were paying Bill Royce more than they were paying me, he said, was because Bill had a wife and a child. It didn't take him long to realize that this wasn't an acceptable excuse. Maybe it was the look on my face.

Ralph quickly changed gears. He told me how much he and Chuck and the others valued me, my work, and my time with *Tiger Beat*. "We will double your salary immediately. Just tell me you'll stay on as editor," he begged. While I had never dreamed I'd be presented such an offer, I was mentally prepared to say goodbye—no ifs, ands, or buts. Don and I had rehearsed my response. I was taking a stand for justice.

At the end of our conversation, Ralph suggested I work another two months so I would be eligible for one hundred percent of my profit sharing. I agreed and worked through the end of March. The last issue of Tiger Beat I worked on was published in May of 1972.

People often ask me *why* I left *Tiger Beat* when they had clearly shown me that they wanted me to stay. Looking back, it's evident to me that a big part of my decision was the control my husband had in our relationship. I think when Don and I began dating in 1968, I was "on the rebound." Maurice Gibb had just dumped me, and I was searching for validation—proof that someone could love me. I also longed for a "normal," non-Hollywood life, since I equated my being tossed away by

Maurice with his rock star status, and I feared that all Hollywood people were just as mean and shallow as Maurice had proved to be.

My break-up with Maurice had more than broken my heart; it broke my spirit. Before, I'd always been in control of my life, and I was successful because of my drive and my confidence. Somehow, I lost much of that confidence, and quite a lot of myself, when Maurice left my life. It would be years before I would become myself again. In the meantime, there was Don. We'd been friends since high school, had worked together at Disneyland, and he'd just returned from military service in Vietnam. He personified stability to me, at a time when the world felt unstable and a little bit cruel.

When I think back on this now, it's with some irony, because while Don meant "stability" to me when we were young, it was I who became the true breadwinner once we became a real couple.

Leaving *Tiger Beat* was one of the hardest things I've ever done. I rationalized my decision by telling myself, "I'll get a job at *Sunset* magazine," which had offices in Menlo Park, near where we'd settled in Northern California. Don had gone to work in a nearby sporting goods store, just as he'd planned to.

I did get an interview with the editor of *Sunset,* and while he was very gracious to me, it came down to money. Laufer had been paying me a way-above-average salary, including my car lease, expense account, and free reign as editor. The *Sunset* editor was frank. "I can hire a Stanford graduate for $400 a month," he told me. "We can't afford you." Even though I told him the money was not the issue, it was the end of the discussion.

From that point on, I worked low-paying, fairly boring jobs, and Don and I brought in about the same paycheck. Did that make our marriage stronger? No, it just kept us going, living day to day.

I never again found a job as satisfying on every level as my time as editor of *Tiger Beat*. I often regretted having left, but I tried to make myself believe I was just as happy in my new life. It still stung that they'd treated me so unfairly after I'd poured my heart into "their" magazine for six years.

Laudy, Sharon, and I remained close friends over the years, and had reunions every few years, no matter where we were living. In 2005, they flew to Denver, where I was enjoying the best years of my life. My second husband, Tony, and I had married in 1980, and in the early 1980s we'd adopted our sons, Matthew and Michael. During that long girls-of-*Tiger Beat* weekend, Laudy shared something that finally made me feel better about my long-ago decision to get out of the Laufer business.

"You know," she told me, "when you weren't in the office, Ralph and Chuck never referred to you by name. They called you 'the Starfucker.'"

My heart sank. I was shocked, and in some ways, I couldn't believe it. Deep down, I knew Laudy was telling me the truth about this horrible, shameful nickname. And the worst thing about it was that the nasty name Ralph and Chuck had secretly called me was totally untrue. Other than my two brief affairs, both of which I knew as romantic relationships, I'd spent a lot of years gently saying "No, thanks" to a lot of horny rock stars.

Laudy's awful admission set me free, in a way. I'd regretted my decision about leaving *Tiger Beat* for a long, long time, but I realized that my exit was more than just me standing up for women's rights. It was a kind of self-preservation.

I really believe that everything in our lives happens for a reason. If I hadn't been married to Don for nine years, had an amicable divorce and no children, I never would have moved to Salt Lake City and never would have met Tony, who taught me what real love is like. We'd never have raised the two sons God chose for us, and I'd never have known what it was like to raise a family. My decision to leave the Laufer compound led me to where I am today. How can I regret anything that brought me the best thirty-seven years of my life?

I was blessed that I shared my *Tiger Beat* years with genuine people like Laudy and Sharon; Bobby Sherman, Davy Jones, Peter Tork; and all the readers of *Tiger Beat*. I'm blessed that I now share my life with Tony, our sons and our many friends. In the end, all of my life has been much more than I dreamed of during those carefree days selling orange juice at Disneyland.

If you enjoyed this book…

You can find Ann online at Facebook.com/annmoses

And please visit me at www.annmoses.com for all the stories that didn't fit in this memoir. There are loads of them, and I'll be spilling them over the coming months, plus never-before-seen photos! I'm hoping this will open a dialogue between you and me – if you have any questions, I hope to have a regular Q & A feature, so send your questions to annimoses@annmoses.com!

Acknowledgments

It goes without saying that I couldn't have written this book if I hadn't enjoyed the company of your many "faves"—too numerous to mention—all those years ago. The publicists and promoters who made working with those stars a possibility helped enormously. At the very top of that list is Rick Picone. Of course, my colleagues Laudy Powell, Sharon Lee, Ralph Benner, Norbert Jobst, Robert Custer, David Meyer, Kenny Lieu, Patt Frankenfield, Lynn Kahan, and Charles Laufer helped me learn the pop star biz or worked alongside me to bring *Tiger Beat* to you each month.

I'm indebted to my parents, Jack and Rosemary Moses. They raised me in a household where racism and hate were unacceptable, gave me encouragement that knew no bounds and were the best role models for great parenting one could ever hope for.

I'm grateful for Laurie Jacobson, Ken Sharpe, Chris Campion and Adam Parfrey for encouragement and guidance during the writing and publishing process. Stephen Levandowski, Karen Green, Carol Davis, and Pat Skolout all read early drafts and offered input and suggestions. Jim Mullahy helped bring my brother's story about guarding the Beatles full circle, and Teri Pierce provided the final puzzle piece to the story of my first true love.

Thank you to Mindy Evanson, Meghan Brozanic, Mark Pringle, Barry Hoskyns, Roger Semon, Bill Bram, Mikky Jones and Tracy Thomas. How I wish I could fly you all to Hollywood to meet your faves and then take you to lunch at the Yankee Peddler.

Andrew Sandoval, Tiffany DuFoe, Terry DuFoe, David Ghosty Wills, Ken Mills, Sarah Clarke, Bonnie Verrico, Mary Cherry, Suzanne Gee, Anita Weinberg and Mark Easter/Alan Jeffries helped me connect with *Tiger Beat* readers from the early days and beyond. Steven Novak designed fabulous cover art, Russ Kazmierczak produced the gorgeous trailer, and Barry Haldeman and Jeffrey Riffer handled all the legal mumbo jumbo with precision. Props go out to Sean Barclay for your kindness, and I'm holding out hope that we will work together one day.

A special thank you to Ralph Benner, who emailed Laudy in 2012 to say, "I hear Ann is writing a book about her *Tiger Beat* days. Good for her. So many others have done this with little success." That snarky note made me work harder than ever on this project. You, my longtime friends and loyal readers, will make or break his prediction.

Endless gratitude goes to my friend and editor Ann Wicker, who was instrumental in bringing this memoir to life. I met Ann, with help from Larry Page and Sergey Brin, in 2012 when Mindy Evanson Googled "Ann Moses Tiger Beat" and Ann Wicker's blog post about the death of Davy Jones popped up. "When I was 12, in my daydreams, I was Ann Moses," Ann Wicker wrote. "She always wore groovy clothes, white or light pink lipstick and had bright red hair. She talked to Davy Jones and Micky Dolenz on the phone. Bobby Sherman called her 'babe.' She was cool."

I was absolutely blown away to discover there were people out there who actually knew who I was and remembered my work from the 60s and early 70s. It got me to thinking that maybe all those people who'd been telling me for years "You've got to write a book!" weren't crazy after all.

I contacted Ann, a journalist who'd written for magazines, published a book on music, and edited many novels. It quickly became clear that together, we could tell my story about "the good old days" at *Tiger Beat*. In the process, Ann and I became close friends. We took week-long writing trips to Santa Fe, New Mexico, Sedona, Arizona and Charleston, South Carolina, where we strung together my memories of David Cassidy, Mark Lindsay, and of course Elvis Presley into a narrative we both hope you'll enjoy.

A final shout-out goes to my newest friend, Robrt Pela, who did the final edit on the manuscript and suggested the title. Robrt and his husband, Todd Grossman, have become my and my own husband's dearest friends. Robrt, who thanked me in the acknowledgements of his own first book 15 years before we met, says he owes his 35-year career in journalism to me.

"I was speaking at ASU's school of journalism one day last year," Robrt told me when we met, "and one of the students asked why I went into journalism. I replied, 'When I was 9 years old, I wanted to be Ann Moses.'" When the student asked Robrt if he'd ever written me a thank-you note, it occurred to him that he hadn't, and he should. This time, Mark Zuckerberg brought me together with an old friend I'd never met before.

There are so many of you out there (who knew there were so many males who read *Tiger Beat*? I didn't until now!) who've "known" me for so long. I hope this book will bridge the gap of time and distance between us, and prove to you that, although we haven't yet met, I was thinking about you all, way back when it was my job to help make your dreams come true.

Ann Moses
Gilbert, AZ,
April, 2017

First, I want to thank Ann Moses Marino, who was a hero of mine when I was young, and her husband, Tony Marino, for their confidence in me. Back in the day, I wanted to *be* Ann Moses of *Tiger Beat* and hang out with the Monkees, Bobby Sherman, Herman's Hermits, Kurt Russell, and the rest. I never dreamed I'd have the privilege of working with Ann on her memoir of those heady days. Her friendship has been a great gift.

I need to thank many people for their support, even though I'm afraid I'll forget someone. My Davidson Brain Trust always comes through, and for this project, I especially want to thank Bo Phillips, Dickson Phillips, Terry Hummel, Nancy Northcott, Van Garrison, Debbie Darden, and Staley Nance.

Thanks, too, to Donna Campbell, Georgann Eubanks, Cathy Anderson, John Jeeter, Terry Hoover, Emily Seelbinder, Cindy Campbell, Paula Connolly, Don Dixon, Dawn Cotter, Linda Hutchinson, Linda Dennehy, Carol Koball, Ellen Adams, Steve Stoeckel, Pat Walters, Jamie Hoover, Peg Robarchek, Betsy Bevan Thorpe, Jean Nantz Walkup, Linda Brown, David Walters, and John and Shalini Morris.

Most of all, thanks and love to my husband, Mark Williams, who is my biggest fan and supporter and who encourages me every step of the way.

Ann Wicker

Charlotte, NC, March, 2017

Printed in Dunstable, United Kingdom

66477421R00180